54.399498°N 0.491953°W

Copyright © Skyshots Imagery Ltd

First published in Great Britain in 2019 by The Town That Never Was .

All rights reserved. No part of this publication may be reproduced, stored in a retrieval system, or transmitted in any form or by any means, electronic mechanical, photocopying recording or otherwise, without the prior written permission of the publishers.

A catalogue record for this book is available from the British library.
ISBN 978-1-5272-3843-5

Every effort has been made to fulfil the requirements with regard to any copyright material.
The author and publisher will be glad to rectify any omission the earliest opportunity.

All original documents and images in this book are reproduced with the kind permission of;
North Yorkshire County Record Office
Skyshots Imagery Ltd. private collection
All other images and documents reproduced are in the public domain.

This is a work of non-fiction. No names have been changed, no characters invented, no events fabricated.
The work has been created through extensive analysis of the archive and internet research by the authors.

Cover: Original brick from Ravenscar Brickworks
Rear Cover: Gold sovereign struck in 1896

THE REMARKABLE AND INTRIGUING TRUE STORY OF RAVENSCAR THE TOWN THAT NEVER WAS

www.thetownthatneverwas.co.uk

ROADS THAT WAIT FOR HOUSES

BY A PERIPATETIC,
YORKSHIRE POST,
THURSDAY AUGUST 14TH, 1913

In Ravenscar I came across a man one day.

He was standing on the road staring at the scenery.

"Beastly day, isn't it?" said I.

"Rotten," said he, "but only the usual Ravenscar weather.

See that land?"

I nodded.

"Well," that's mine. I helped to pay for this road. Why?
Because I once lunched, not wisely but too well.
I saw visons of stately manors standing there. I nodded my head and the auctioneer's hammer fell.

"Would you," he added wistfully, "like to buy a bit of land? You can have it at your own price."

I left him there staring at those "desirable building plots"!

Extracted as written in the Yorkshire Post

39th Sale

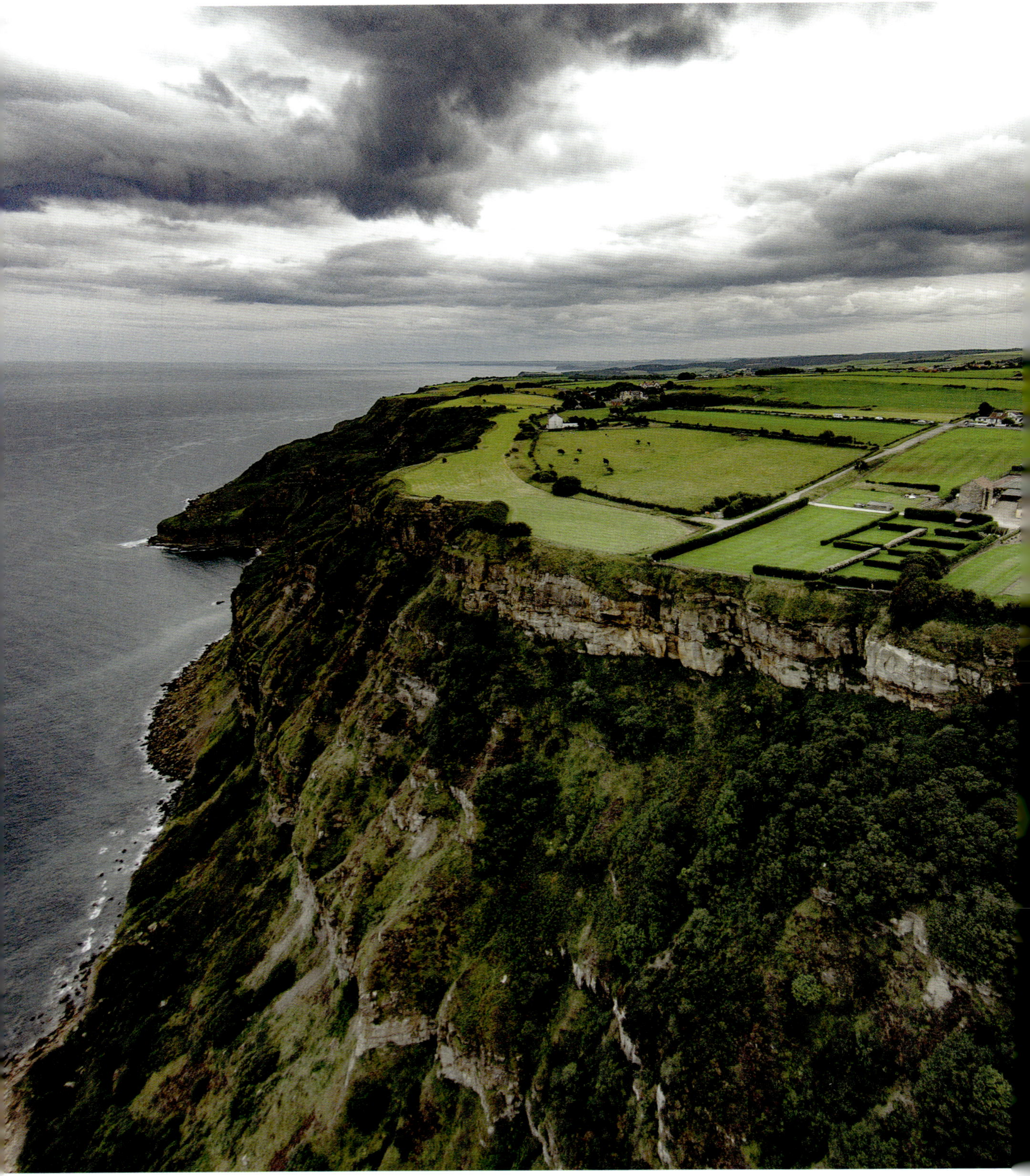

Preface

Ravenscar is a tiny coastal village between Scarborough & Whitby with beautiful views along the North Yorkshire coast. This location rivals any coastal and moorland area in the UK in its scenery and diversity, retaining an unmolested beauty and tranquillity.

Let us take you back to a time where most houses did not have running water or electricity; Oscar Wilde was on trial for his homosexuality and Queen Victoria had just surpassed her grandfather, George III as the longest reigning monarch in British history.

In 1896, in a village that was still known as Peak, grounds were being dug up to lay drains and sewers, whilst roads were being built in preparation for the newest Victorian seaside town which was intended to rival Blackpool.

This is the story of a town that was intended to be built, the vision of a group of influential men of the day, over a century ago.

The obvious question is, 'Why was the town never built?' In this story we give you an insight into the facts and we explain the truth behind some of the myths which have existed for some time.

We have undertaken extensive research to get to this stage, but we are sure that there is still more to tell.

We want the story to continue …. If you manage to discover more facts and can add to the story, please do contact us. Perhaps one of your relatives was involved in the planning of the town? Perhaps one of them bought a plot, built a house or even just holidayed at the hotel in its hey-day?

We would be delighted to hear your stories….

Visit the website at www.thetownthatneverwas.co.uk

The story intertwines with significant people and events at that time. It is a story that leaves much to the imagination of what might have been.

INTRODUCTION

Beside the seaside, beside the sea!

The British seaside resort was a creation of the eighteenth century, when it was believed that both the drinking of, and bathing in sea water was a cure for many maladies. The growth of seaside resorts on a grand scale began with the railway age and was brought to fulfilment by the middle class throughout the latter years of the nineteenth century.
As the railway system developed throughout Britain, the ease and relatively low cost of getting to the coast also meant that working-class families were able to benefit particularly in the form of day trips.
The seaside resorts had their own unique culture of brass bands, Punch and Judy shows, music halls, fairground attractions and such like which provided a carnival-like atmosphere. This in turn stimulated the latent fun, laughter and suspension of inhibitions which the likes of Charles Dickens, Charles Kingsley and Lewis Carrol celebrated to their readers.

The developing resorts fought against the respectability and fear of embarrassment that were strong in Victorian culture. Escape to the seaside brought to the surface the uneasiness about morality and identity which were so pervasive in Victorian life. There was a stark contrast between middle-class ladies in their bathing machines, who took great pains to ensure that they could swim in the sea without being seen, and the working-class young men who used the telescopes on the pier to catch a glimpse as the ladies lowered themselves into the sea!

Those who envisaged the development of Ravenscar, or Peak as it was known then, saw the opportunity for the town to stand alongside Blackpool and Scarborough. There was high demand for more seaside resorts from those who laboured in those dark satanic mills of Yorkshire.
During the Industrial Revolution, the tradition of the "Wakes week" was adapted into a regular summer holiday, particularly in the North of England. Industrialised areas such as Bradford and Leeds nominated a Wakes week during which the local factories, wool and cotton mills, collieries and other industries closed for a week.

There was a long-held belief amongst the working classes of the north of England in the benefits of bathing in the sea during the months of August and September.

The wide-ranging social impact of the Industrial Revolution included the remaking of the working class as new technologies appeared. The changes resulted in the creation of a larger, increasingly professional middle class, the decline of child labour and the dramatic growth of a consumer-based, material culture. Opportunities for all…

On the Sands at Blackpool — Hedley Fitton, '95

John Manners the Marques of Granby By Joshua Reynolds

1764

HE LOVED IT SO MUCH HE BOUGHT IT

Peak was a tiny collection of workers cottages, scattered and subservient to the only building of any significance, which stood alone and prominent on the headland, Peak House. This building had housed the various owners of the alum works who had been operating at Peak since the 17th-century. A significant amount of the area had been affected by this process, which involved constructing 100 feet tall stacks of burning shale and consistently and continuously fuelling them with firewood for months. However, in the pre-industrial age, alum was in demand globally as it was essential in the textile industry as a fixative for dyes.

In 1763 Captain William Child of the renowned family 'Child & Co', one of the oldest private banking institutions, returned to England at the end of the Seven Years' War.

Captain William Child married and chose to make his home in Yorkshire. He bought all of the properties and a significant amount of land in Peak, including the alum works. In 1774 he completed the work of rebuilding the original Peak House into the style of a large Palladian villa. This was the start of the building that subsequently became the Raven Hall Hotel which still stands there today. William and his wife Anne made their home there and brought up their three children, William, Mary and Anne.

ABOVE: Original title deed for Peak Estate signed & sealed by Capt William Child 1763
FACING: Antique pub sign depicting the Marquess of Granby

Last Orders Please

During the Seven Years' War Capt William Child had distinguished himself, most notably at the battle of Warburg which was fought on 31 July 1760. The Battle was a victory for the Hanoverians and the British against the French. His commanding officer, General John Manners, Marquess of Granby, was a genuine British military hero. He was one of the first who understood the importance of welfare and morale for the troops. He is probably best known today for being popularly supposed to have more pubs named after him than any other person - due, it is said, to his practice of setting up old soldiers of his regiment as publicans when they were too old to serve any longer.

While leading a charge at the Battle of Warburg, he is said to "have lost his hat and wig, forcing him to salute his commander without them".

This incident is commemorated by the British Army tradition today that non-commissioned officers and troopers of the Blues and Royals are the only soldiers of the British Army who may salute without wearing headdress.

Capt. William Child also served alongside the illegitimate son of the Marquees of Granby, Capt. George Manners, at that time the MP for Scarborough. We can only speculate if that connection made on the battlefield was what brought William Child to Yorkshire.

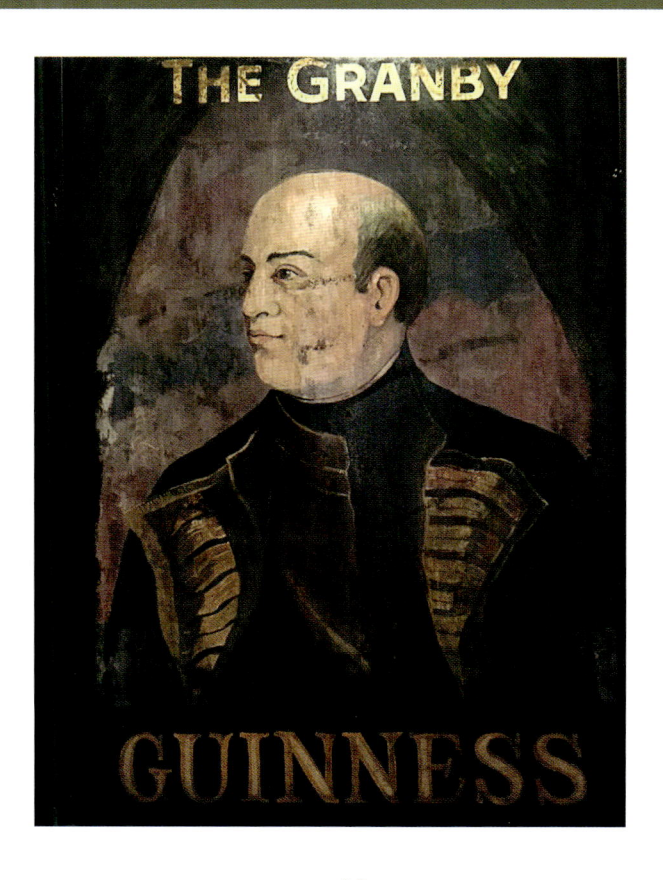

Anne Child, the youngest daughter of Capt. William Childs and his wife, married Admiral Richard Willis in 1793 and together they moved to Petworth in Sussex. Richard Willis was the 4th son of the renowned Dr Francis Willis who is credited with curing the madness of King George III.

Dr Francis Willis' treatment of the King included many of the standard methods of the period, such as coercion, restraint in a straitjacket and blistering of the skin, but he is reputed to have shown more kindness and consideration for his patient than had previously been given. The King's recovery made Willis' national reputation and he became a British celebrity. He was reputedly rewarded by the King with £1,000 a year for 21 years.

But for the union between Anne Child & Admiral Richard Willis, Ravenhill Hall may have continued as a family home for years to come. The future was set, when on the 4th March 1799, at Petworth in Sussex, Anne gave birth to her third son, Richard Child Willis.

Following the death of her mother in 1829, Anne Willis (née Child) inherited Ravenhill Estate. Her father had planned carefully and left detailed instructions to the executors of his will. On his wife's death, he detailed how his estate was to be divided.

His leasehold properties in London went equally to his children William Gilbert Child and Anne Willis, and his freehold properties in Scarborough went to his daughter Mary Child. The Estate at Peak and his East India stock and bank annuities were placed in trust such that the rents and income arising from them went to his daughter Mary so long as she was unmarried, and then they went to his son William and William's heir 'begotten of a European Woman but not of a Black or Mulatto'. Should he not have such heirs, the income was to go to Mary and Anne equally, and after the last of them should die, to the male heir of Mary, and failing that, to the male heir of Anne. Neither William Gilbert Child nor Mary Willis had any heirs so Richard, Anne's son, ultimately became the sole heir.

FACING: Actual will of Admiral Richard Wiillis, the husband of Anne Child. ABOVE King George III

Extracted from the Registry of the Prerogative Court of Canterbury

This is the last Will

and Testament of me Richard Willis Petworth in the County of Sussex Esq. Rear Admiral of His Majestys Navy I give and bequeath all my money securities for money household furniture Goods Chattels and personal Estate and Effects whatsoever and wheresoever (subject nevertheless to the payment of my just Debts and funeral and testamentary expences) unto my dear Wife Ann Willis her Executors Administrators and Assigns and I appoint her my said Wife sole Executrix of this my Will In Witness whereof I have hereunto set my hand and seal this twenty fifth Day of April in the Year of our Lord one thousand eight hundred and twenty eight — (Richd Willis (LS)) Signed Sealed Published and Declared by the sd

A DIVINE in his GLORY!!
*The business of his Church – he did by Proxy.
And loved all Doxies – but the Ortho-doxy*

A Divine in his Glory, a caricature by Isaac Cruikshank

1836

NOT ENTIRELY CLERICAL

Richard Willis was from this wealthy, notable family of the highest standing in society. He graduated from University College, Oxford in 1817, completed an MA in 1822 and two years later completed a postgraduate BD Bachelor of Divinity which was the highest-ranking bachelor's degree available at Oxford and Cambridge, outranking a PhD. It required a significant dedication to and knowledge of Christian Theology.

Between his studies he was ordained in 1822, and in 1823 he became the Perpetual Curate of North Stoke in Sussex. Perpetual in this sense, meant that once licensed, he could only be removed by his diocesan bishop through the ecclesiastical courts. Curate meant that he was licensed by the diocesan bishop to provide 'cure of souls' for the people of the district or parish. Richard went on to marry Frances Hale in 1826 and to add to his distinguished position, he played first-class cricket for Sussex and made an appearance for England.

Richard liked the good life, including drink and women. William Child, Richard's grandfather, had recognised and was aware of the wayward tendencies of his grandson. Fate had determined that he was to be the only living heir in the family by the time that his mother passed away in 1835. However, to safeguard against these circumstances and to protect the Peak Estate from being squandered by Richard, William had left the estate in fee tail, meaning that each generation only had a life interest in it before it then passed to each subsequent heir or into the hands of the executors.

Fee tail denotes passing by inheritance from one generation to the next. Each beneficiary has no right to transfer, sell or mortgage such property, they are merely a 'tenant' during their lifetime.

Richard Child Willis was not content with only a life interest in the estate and an income of £2,000 a year, so he contested his grandfather's will. He wanted outright ownership. Due to a technicality in the wording of the will, following a lengthy court battle, Ravenhill Hall passed to Richard. The Court of Chancery found that the will was worded so that it devised the Estate to Ann Willis' heir (singular), rather than her heirs (plural) - or in other words, to her immediate heir, Richard, rather than all her future heirs in whatever generation they may be.

By 1837 legal matters were settled and Richard and his wife set about extending and renovating Ravenhill Hall, to create a new neo-classical mansion house. It was fitted out and furnished to the highest standards of the day. Richard blasted out the cliff face below the mansion and created the most magnificent battlements and gardens. Nowadays these may be seen at the most north-easterly extremity of the grounds of Raven Hall Hotel.

Addicted to gambling and the high life as Richard was, many lurid stories started to emerge about the goings on at Ravenhill Hall which were the talk of the towns of Whitby and Scarborough. However, he had remortgaged the whole Estate and borrowed extensively and by 1840 the party was over. Richard was penniless and in debt. Richard and his wife were predominantly in debt to three eminent London gentlemen: William Hammond, estate agent and auctioneer of 28 Chancery Lane, London; John Allcard, an eminent Quaker banker and stockbroker; and Henry Sykes Thornton, a banker who was the cousin of William Wilberforce, the famous campaigner for the abolition of slavery. The three men were owed approximately £10,400.

Dated 30th November 1851.

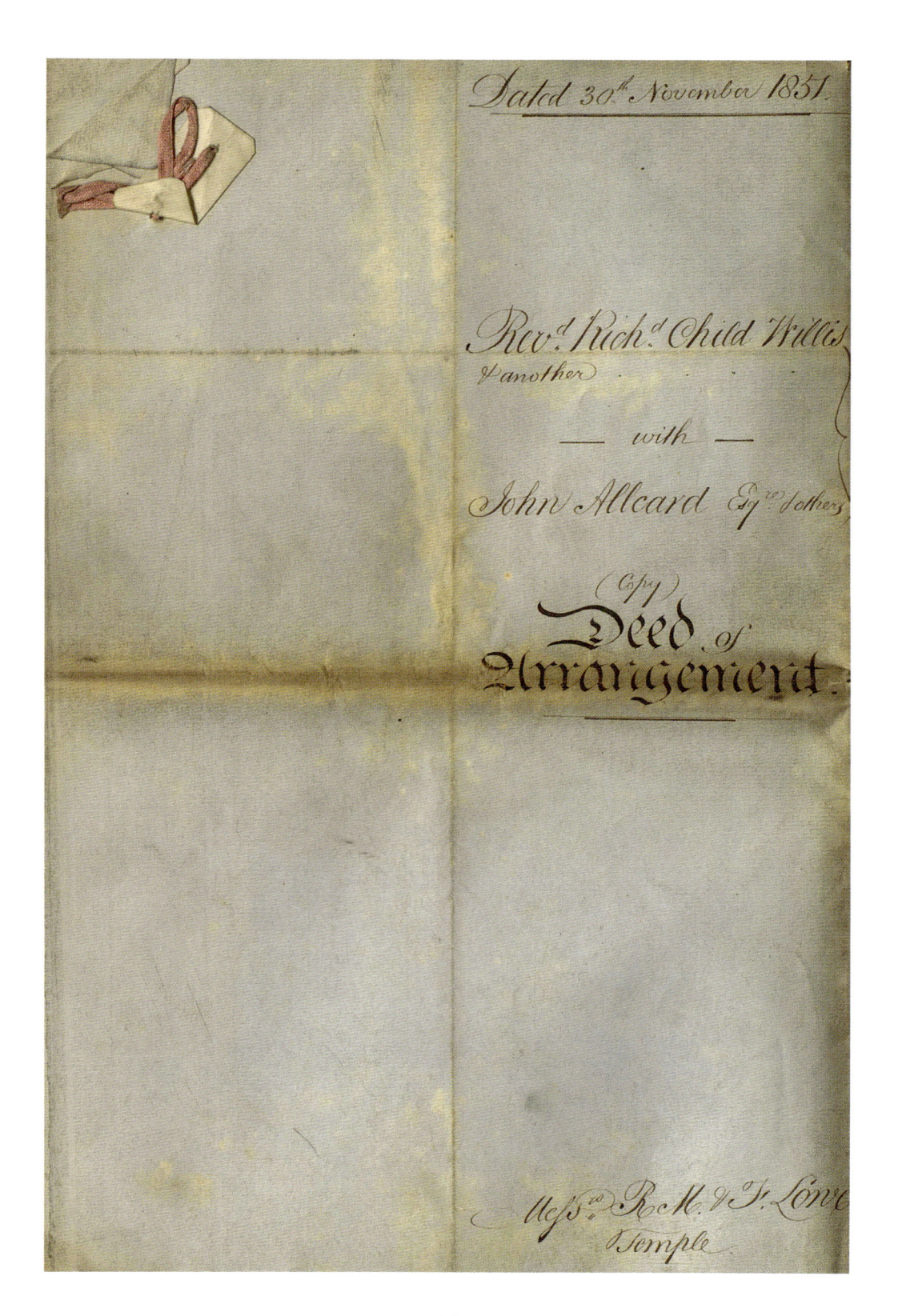

Revd Richd Child Willis
& another

— with —

John Allcard Esqre & others

(Copy)
Deed of Arrangement

Messrs R. M. & F. Lowe
Temple

Cash in the Attic

Mr. HAMMOND begs respectfully to give Notice that he has had the Elegant FITTINGS and FURNITURE of RAVENHILL HALL REMOVED to the NEW HALL at SCARBOROUGH, TO BE SOLD BY AUCTION on Wednesday, December 30th, and Two Following Days, at Twelve precisely; comprising Elegant Four-post Bedstead-, and Damask Hangings ; superior | Bedding; Mahogany French Bedsteads; Handsome Winged Wardrobe; Marble Top Washhand Stand; Spanish Mahogany Toilet Tables ; Large Cheval and Dressing Glasses Pedestal Cupboard ; Patent Portable Water Closet ; Drawers ; costly Dining and Drawing Boom Suites, in Fine Spanish Mahogany and Solid Rose- wood, of Chairs, Couches, and Sofas, in Morocco and Chintz; Console Table, Plate Glass; Devonport's Tardiniere. Loo, and Card Tables; Pedestal Sideboards; Patent Coal Boxes; Extending Dining Table. ; Pair of Massive Running Sideboards ; Secretaries; Easy Chairs ; Fittings of Hall ; Dinner, Tea, and Dessert Services ; Capital Culinary Articles, etc. To be Viewed Three Days prior to the Sale by Catalogues only, at 6d. each, to be had at the Royal Hotel, Bell and Talbot Inn, Scarborough -, York Tavern, George and Black Swan Inn, York; Angel at Whitby; Talbot Inn, Malton ; the New Hall of the Odd- Fellows' Lodge, Scarborough ; and at Mr. Hammond's, Estate Agency Offices, 30, Bell-Yard, and 28, Chancery -Lane,
London. N.B. The Noble MANSION and ESTATE of about 300 ACRES is to be SOLD BY AUCTION IN APRIL NEXT.

LEEDS INTELLIGENCER, 19 DECEMBER 1840

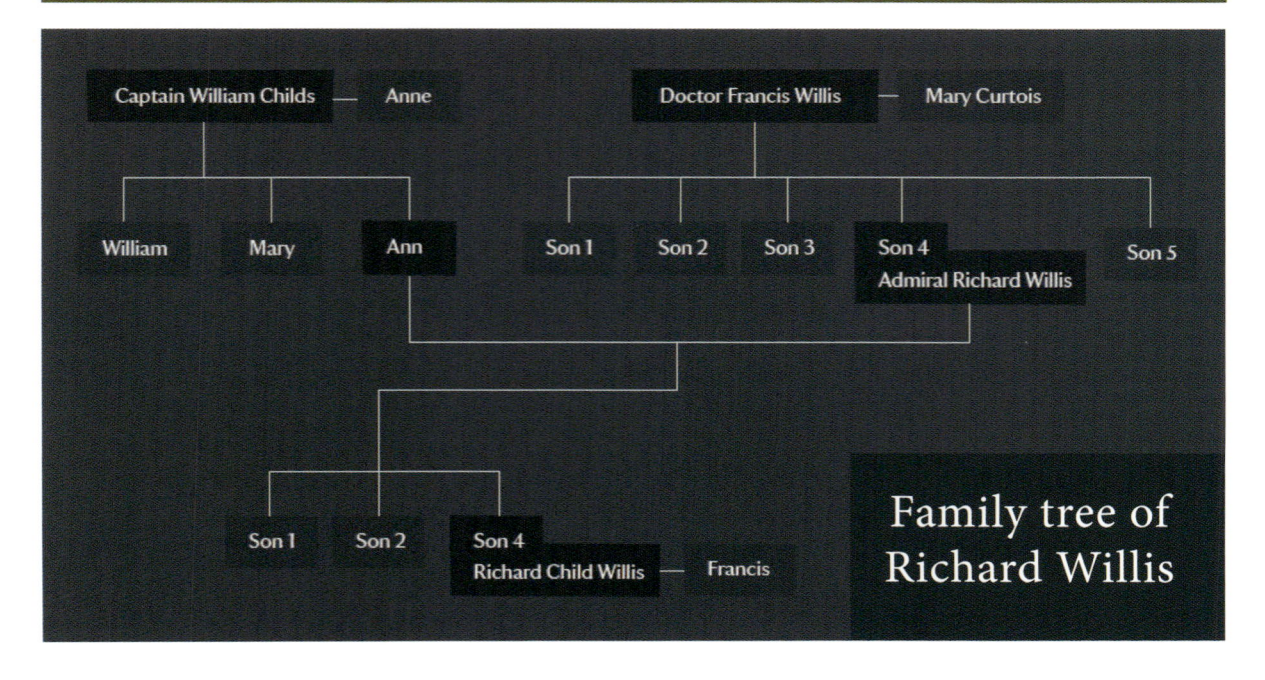

Family tree of Richard Willis

- Captain William Childs — Anne
  - William
  - Mary
  - Ann
- Doctor Francis Willis — Mary Curtois
  - Son 1
  - Son 2
  - Son 3
  - Son 4 Admiral Richard Willis
  - Son 5

Ann & Admiral Richard Willis:
- Son 1
- Son 2
- Son 4 Richard Child Willis — Francis

William Hammond was a successful gentleman who was running a large prominent estate agency business from his London Offices, 28 Chancery Lane, London. He had taken a charge over the Estate at Peak to secure his loan. Recognising that there was little prospect of the Reverend and his wife repaying the debt, William Hammond, in his professional capacity and as mortgagee, made plans to dispose of the Estate by auction.

He began extensively cataloguing and advertising the Estate. This first sale of all the furniture, fixtures and fittings that had been removed from Ravenhill Hall was held in Scarborough in December 1840.

Richard and his wife moved to Haddenham in Buckinghamshire where Richard acted as curate for his cousin who was temporarily suspended from his duties, having admitted to visiting a brothel in Aylesbury and being drunk both in the pulpit and in a hayrick! William Hammond and the other creditors entered into several agreements with Richard and Frances to try and structure debt repayments whilst Ravenhill Hall remained empty and unsold.

In April 1841 and again in August 1842, the whole Estate was put up for auction but failed to attract any buyers. In 1846 William Hammond offered the Estate for rent but he still could not find to find anyone willing to take on what was now becoming a liability. In 1850 he finally formally foreclosed on the mortgage. He settled with John Allcard and Henry Sykes Thornton and became the outright owner of the Ravenhill Hall Estate and its 800 acres. He decided therefore that it would become his country retreat.

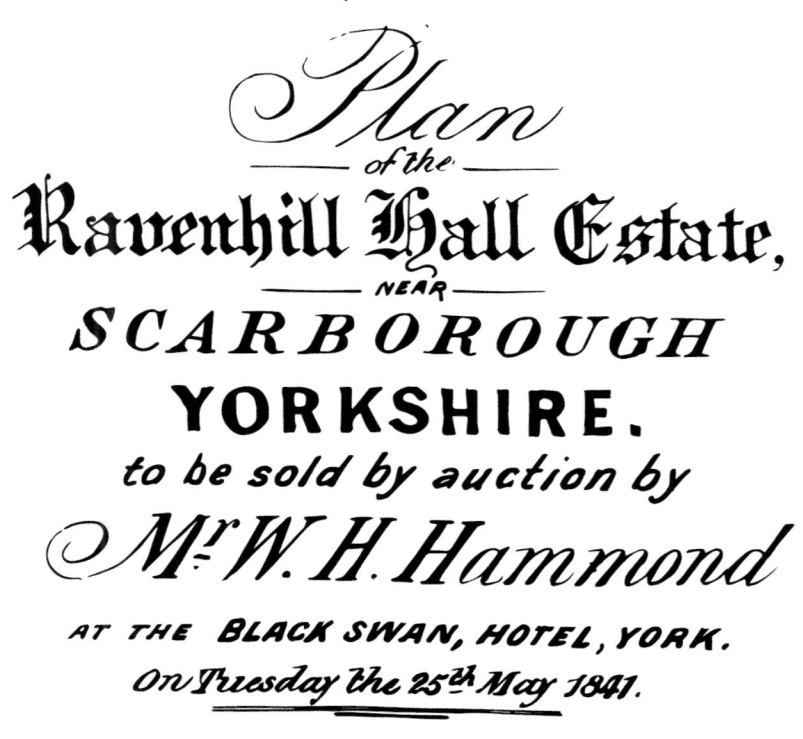

Plan of the
Ravenhill Hall Estate,
— NEAR —
SCARBOROUGH
YORKSHIRE.
to be sold by auction by
Mr W. H. Hammond
AT THE BLACK SWAN, HOTEL, YORK.
On Tuesday the 25th May 1841.

From Scarborough.

As for the Reverend Richard Child Willis, Doctor of Divinity, he became the Chaplin to the Sheppy workhouse in 1849. However, in stark contrast to his apparent respectability, he was still managing to live the high life. He was making quite a reputation for himself in London. He would check into the top hotels in London at the time, such as Hatchett's of Piccadilly and the Sablonnerie Hotel in Leicester Square. The Archbishop had heard about these activities and was not best pleased with the young Reverend. He had statements of indisputable authority that Reverend Childs had lived for seven weeks at a hotel in London under the name of Captain Child, (reference to his grandfather no doubt), before leaving the female who he had arrived with to pay the bill, and that this said Doctor regularly speculated on the horses!

Richard continued to trade on his position and connections, as well as the reputation of both of his distinguished grandfathers. He would check into hotels with different women for a few nights or a few weeks and run up tremendous bills. He would then present a cheque for payment drawn against accounts with banks with which he had no accounts.

He would write a cheque for an amount higher than the bill and request cash for the balance. Eventually his fraudulent lifestyle caught up with him. The Society for the Protection of Licensed Victuallers had in effect brought a group action against Richard, such was the extent of his fraudulent activity. In April 1850, in the central criminal court, he was found guilty of obtaining money by means of false cheques.

The recorder in passing sentence said that the prisoner had been convicted, upon the most satisfactory evidence, of obtaining money by false pretences, and the evidence left no doubt as to the fraudulent character of his dealings for some considerable time. He thought it right to inform him that for this offence he was liable to be transported for seven years; and although the Court would not proceed to that extremity upon the present occasion, it would most undoubtedly have done so if there had been a conviction upon the other indictments. It had been urged on his behalf that he had filled a high position in society, but this was rather an aggravation than a mitigation of his offence, as it was his duty to have shown a better example to others who were less educated, or who had more temptation to commit such an offence. The learned Judge then sentenced the prisoner to be imprisoned and kept to hard labour in the House of Correction in Coldbath Fields Prison in Clerkenwell for one year.

Victorian Punishments

During the nineteenth century, fraud was considered a serious crime punishable by execution, or more commonly by transportation. During the start of the century this was to an American colony and later often to Australia. The prisoner would serve their sentence and then be released, but mostly they would not have the means to get themselves
back to England. Instead, they would start a new life abroad
and hopefully, work and contribute to the colony.
Coldbath Fields Prison, where Richard Willis was sent, was famous for its strict regime of silence and also for its use of the treadmill. The prisoners were forced to climb the equivalent of 8,640 feet daily in non-productive labour.

PRISONERS WORKING AT THE TREAD-WHEEL, AND OTHERS EXERCISING, IN THE 3rd YARD OF THE VAGRANTS' PRISON, COLDBATH FIELDS.
(From a Photograph by Herbert Watkins, 179, Regent Street.)

Central Criminal Court

On April 8 Richard Child Willis, an elderly person of gentlemanly appearance, and a clergyman of the Church of England, surrendered to take his trial upon an indictment for misdemeanour. Mr. Ballantine prosecuted, and Mr. Parry appeared for the defendant. Mr. W. Smith deposed that he was a wine-merchant, carrying on business in Leicester-square, and was acquainted with the prisoner. On the 12th February, 1849, the prisoner produced a cheque for £2 upon Messrs. Drummond and Co., signed by himself, and asked him to cash it, and he accordingly gave him the amount. The cheque was presented, and it turned out that the prisoner kept no account at the bank. Mr. John Cox, cashier of Messrs. Drummond, deposed that the prisoner kept no account at their house. By Mr. Parry.— He knew that the prisoner kept no account with the bank from having examined the books. The books were not here. Mr. Parry submitted that the books themselves ought to have been produced. The Recorder said the case must go to the jury. Mr. Parry addressed them for the defence, and remarked upon the circumstances of the case, and the fact that the prosecutor would have lent the prisoner the money if he had asked him, without the cheque being at all resorted to, and he earnestly called upon the jury, if they could find ground for reasonable doubt as to the intention of the prisoner, that they would give him the benefit of that doubt, and acquit him. The jury wished to be informed of the reason why the charge had not been brought forward before the present time? Mr. Ballantine said the prosecutor was not desirous to prefer any charge. The prisoner was in custody upon some other matter, and Mr. Smith was summoned by the magistrate. The Jury, after a short deliberation, returned a verdict of Not Guilty. The prisoner was then charged, upon another indictment, with obtaining money by false pretences. In this case it appeared that the prisoner went to the Sabloniere Hotel, in Leicester-square, accompanied by a lady, and having dined, he tendered in payment a cheque which was made payable at Messrs. Currie and Co.'s, and received 4l. 15s. 2d. change. It turned out that the cheque was altogether fictitious. The Jury returned a verdict of Guilty. The prisoner was then charged, upon a third indictment. It appeared in this case, that he had gone to Hatchett's Hotel, Piccadilly, and having run up a bill of 3l. 3s. 6d., he gave a cheque for 14l. 13s. 1d., and being known as a customer of the house, no suspicion was entertained, and the difference was handed over to him, the cheque, as in the other cases, turning out to be of no value. The Jury found the prisoner Guilty. Mr. Ballantine stated that there were no less than 12 other charges of a similar character against him. Judgment was respited.

London Standard, Tuesday 09 April 1850

On completion of his sentence Richard was bankrupt and separated from his wife. He returned to the Isle of Sheppey and continued in his ministry where he was apparently very popular. He later became embroiled in further difficulty and litigation with the Archbishop of Oxford when it was discovered that he was living with another woman. In the census of 1861 he was living with Hester (who was then aged 27) and a child, Henry, aged 5 months who is believed to have been their son. Richard died in 1877 aged 77, leaving less than £100 to his unofficial wife, Hester.

Despite his less than orthodox life he was well regarded by his parishioners.Richard's wife, Frances died in 1881, her will instructing that her property was to be distributed among her relations as if she had died intestate without ever having been married.

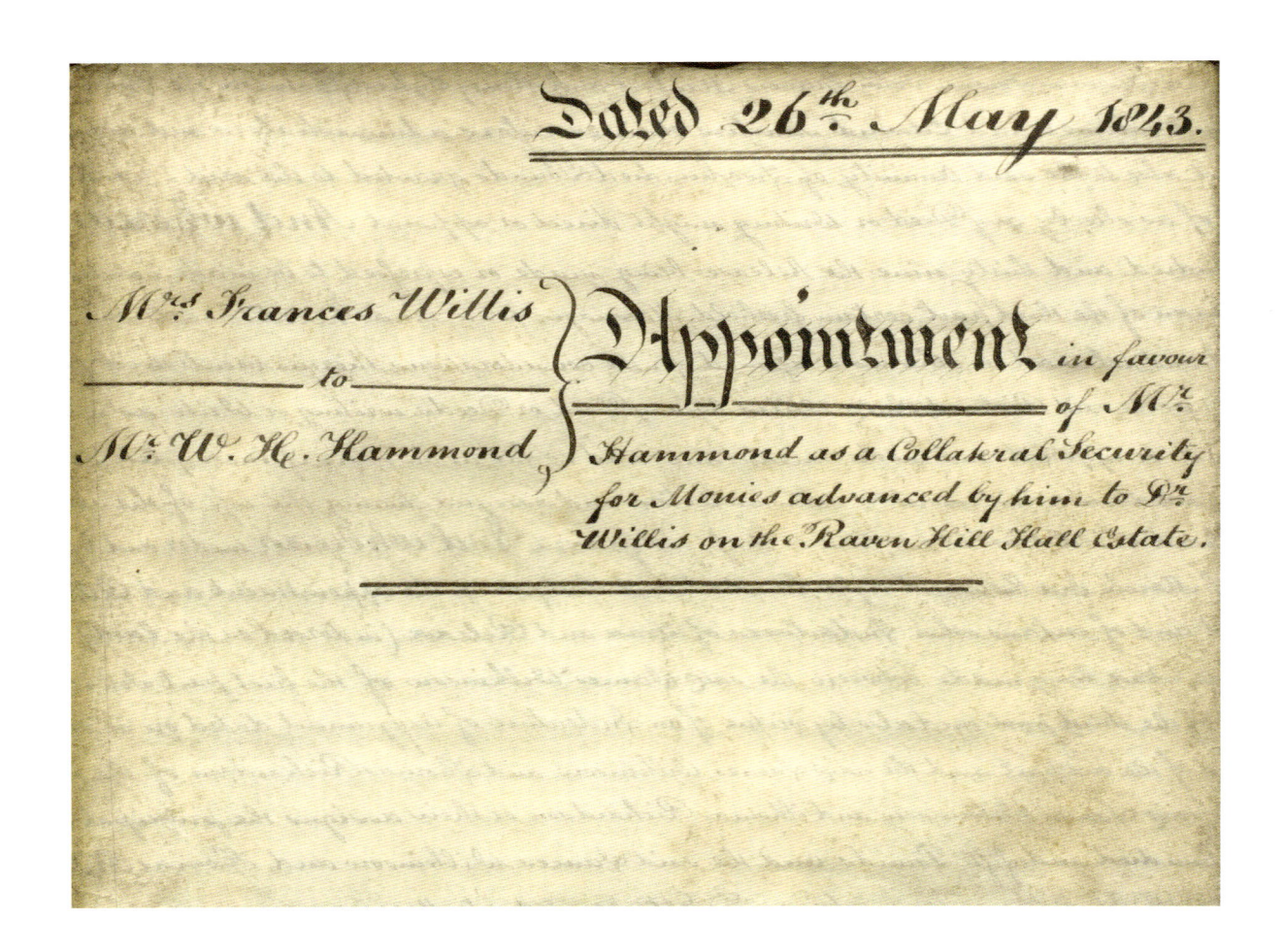

Dated 26th May 1843.

Mrs Frances Willis to Mr W. H. Hammond — *Appointment in favour of Mr Hammond as a Collateral Security for Monies advanced by him to Dr Willis on the Raven Hill Hall Estate.*

Plan of the Ravenhill Hall Estate,
NEAR
SCARBOROUGH YORKSHIRE.
to be sold by auction by
Mr W. H. Hammond
AT THE BLACK SWAN, HOTEL, YORK.
On Tuesday the 25th May 1841.

From Scarborough

Road to Robin Hoods Stoup

Mt Mead

Green Dyke

20·0·0

Spring of Water

Sir W. B. Cook & Co.

47·1·38

Peak Road

R. Campion

Road to Fyling Dales

Lands and Cottages
13·0·9
belonging to Stainton Dale

R. Campion Esq.

Road to Alum Works

8·0·9

0·1·5 Foot

15·0·0

2·3·4

5·1·

Bent Ridge Road

4·2·35   5·2·3

George Ward

30·2·19

1·1·34

0·1·5

2·1·32

4·2·12   6·1·27

1·3·18   Cooks

4·2·0   4·1·34

5·3·31

9·2·38

Ravenhill Hall

3·2·27

5·0·32   6·2·34

7·2·25

6·3·9

4·0·33

Burnt Howe Tumulus

1·3·32   7·1·10

Terrace

Selly Co
5·0·3

'A good type of English gentleman'

With many regrets it is our duty to chronicle the death of the Rev. Dr. Willis, which took place at the Vicarage, Minster, Sheppey, after a short illness, on the 27th ultimo. Dr. Willis was born at Petworth, Sussex, on the 4th of March, 1799, and was the third and only surviving son of the late Rear-Admiral Richard Willis, formerly Port Admiral at Portsmouth, and grandson to Dr. Francis Willis, an English physician of eminence, distinguished for his skill in the treatment of the insane, who was physician to King George the Third, and afterwards had care of the Queen of Portugal. The subject of this notice, the late Rev. Dr. Willis, was in his seventy-eighth year, and was a very remarkable man for his age - energetic, courteous, and accomplished - a good type of the English gentleman and scholar. In youth he became gentleman commoner of the University College, Oxford, and at his thirteenth term he took first class in classics. Somewhere about 1834 he was ordained. But what we more particularly know is that during these last ten years the Rev. Dr. Willis has been vicar of Minster, and well known for his able ministry and preaching. That he was beloved by all who knew him, and by his parishioners, and generally respected, we can testify; assiduous in his duties, his Church was never neglected, and he won the favourable opinion of all classes. To the poor he was ever considerate and kind, and was most respectfully treated by the Archbishop of his diocese (Canterbury). His urbanity, his eloquence as a preacher, and his finished elocution as a reader, drew numbers of people to hear him. Sunday after Sunday many persons from Sheerness wended their way to Minster for the express purpose of listening to the excellent and scholarly discourses of the venerable doctor. In summer the people literally flocked to hear him, so universal was his fame. We sincerely believe that he always lived as he has died, "in peace and harmony with all men," his dying words. It is thought that the worry caused by the litigation brought about by the Bishop of Oxford had a very depressing effect on Dr. Willis, and on the whole hastened his death.

*Sic itur ad astra.

Bucks Herald, 17 February 1877

*Thus one goes to the stars.

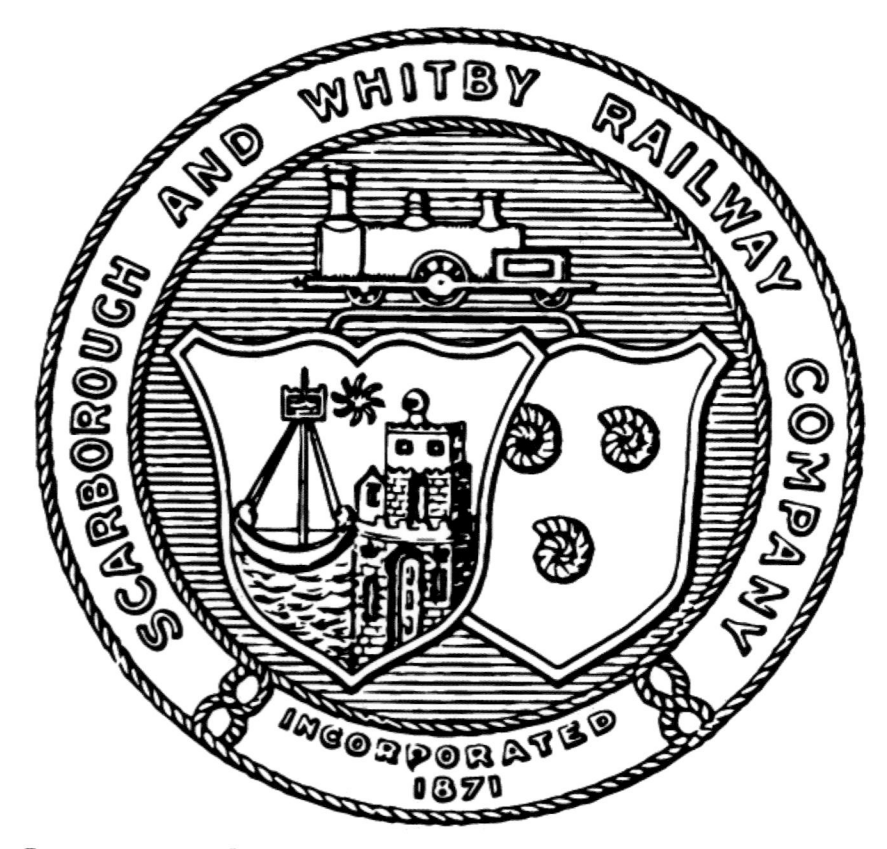

SEAL OF SCARBOROUGH AND WHITBY
RAILWAY COMPANY.

1850 - 1885

THE TRAIN NOW APPROACHING

William Hammond was astute enough to recognise the opportunities for Peak and thereby for himself. The demand for seaside resorts increased dramatically around 1850 on the back of the railway boom which really began in the 1840s. With that came evident commercial potential. Hammond would have identified that if Peak (Ravenscar) had any chance of prosperity in this burgeoning age, it needed a rail link. William Hammond was instrumental in the creation of the Scarborough and Whitby Railway Company, which he first envisaged in 1848. During the Railway mania an Act of Parliament was required to allow the construction of a new railway. He put a bill before Parliament which subsequently received Royal Assent on 5th July 1865, authorising the incorporation of the Scarborough & Whitby Railway. The North-Eastern Railway immediately opposed the formation of this new railway company and its plans to develop a direct route between Scarborough and Whitby. The NER already operated an inland route between the two towns via Malton, but this was 56 miles in length while the proposed new line was only 19 miles. Hammond and others countered this opposition, listing the abundant mineral resources in the district which would support the line's profitability while ensuring that a passenger line ran through Ravenscar.

Unfortunately, sufficient capital to start work couldn't be raised and the permission lapsed. The scheme continued to flounder with numerous false starts due to extreme engineering challenges and exorbitant costs.

There were four attempts made between 1848 and 1881 to establish a railway between Scarborough and Whitby. The combined engineering and topographical challenges, as well as resistance from the NER who were making every effort to retain their monopoly in the area, resulted in each of these attempts failing. Enormous amounts of money were provided (wasted) by speculators and investors, which kept running out. Eugenius Birch, a renowned Victorian engineer, who was one of the main engineers of the East Indian Railway and was instrumental in the design of the Calcutta to Delhi railway and by way of contrast, the ill fated North Bay Pier in Scarborough. He tried but failed to overcome what appeared to have become one of the most challenging stretches of railway ever to be proposed.

In 1880 William Hammond, Ravenscar's main benefactor and now the recognised father of the Scarborough & Whitby Railway Company, resurrected his previous attempt through a further Act of Parliament which received further Royal assent.

He commissioned the engineering firm of Sir Charles Fox & Son of Westminster, who in turn contracted Messrs. John Waddell & Son, an enterprising and respected construction firm who built the Putney Bridge over the River Thames and the Mersey tunnel. By the time the railway was completed in 1885 it had cost £649,813 (which today equates to approximately £80 million) and at almost £30,000 per mile this allegedly, made it the most expensive railway to be built in Britain.

Chainage

In Britain the 'chain' as a form of measurement is no longer used for practical survey work. The chain is a unit of length equal to 66 feet (22 yards). It is subdivided into 100 links or 4 rods. There are 10 chains in a furlong, and 80 chains in one statute mile. However, it survives on the railways of the United Kingdom as a location identifier.

When railways were designed, the location of features such as bridges and stations was indicated by a cumulative longitudinal "mileage", using miles and chains, from a zero point at the origin or headquarters of the railway, or the originating junction of a new branch line. Since railways are entirely linear in topology, the "mileage" or "chainage" is sufficient to identify a place uniquely on any given route. Thus, a certain bridge location may be indicated as x miles and y chains.

Cross Section shewing 9" Sewer 6" Stormwater & 2" Water Main

Robert E Gilmour

Sept. 1900

RAVENSCAR

Crossing at Ravenscar Station

All Iron Pipes in Concrete

Section A.B.

The German Sea

In meteorological terms a 'haar' or sea fret as it's known in Yorkshire is a cold sea fog. It occurs most often on the east coast of England or Scotland between April and September, when warm air passes over the cold North Sea, or as it was known then, the German Sea. (The name North Sea wasn't adopted until the outbreak of the First World War.) They are typically formed over the sea and blown to the land by the wind. This commonly occurs when warmer moist air moves over the relatively cooler North Sea causing the moisture in the air to condense, forming a sea fret.

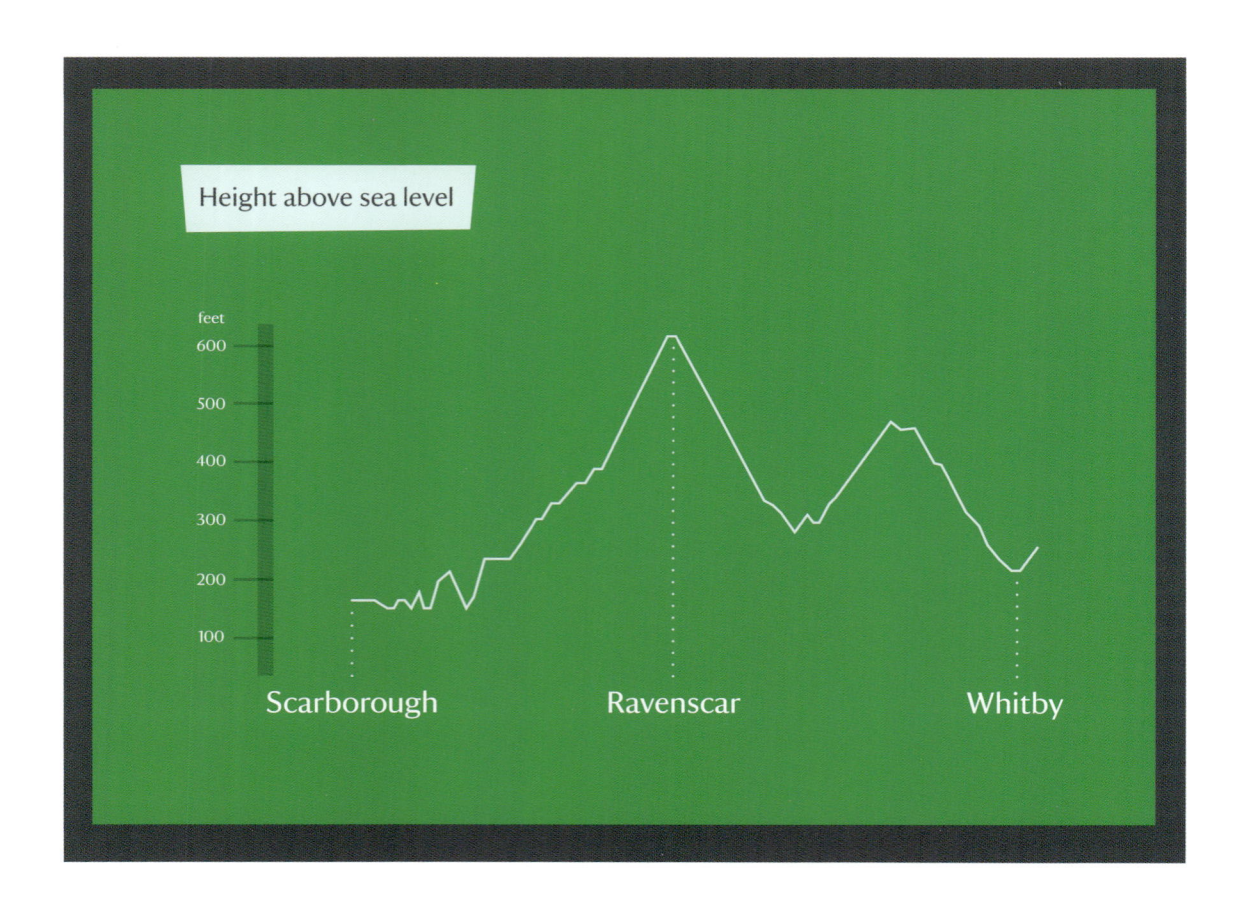

Facing: Heading towards Ravenscar just passing the brickworks climbing the 1-39 gradient.
Above: Gradient diagram of the old railway line, now the 'Cinder Track', a fantastic walk and cycle route.

It has been suggested that William Hammond insisted the tunnel was built as the line passed through his land. A tunnel might seem an obvious way to keep the tracks out of sight on an estate and certainly could satisfy a landowner's wish to retain a favourite vista but there were also disadvantages. It would be costly to the railway company and at Ravenscar a tunnel was completely unnecessary as a cutting would have sufficed. Defining whether the line should proceed by tunnelling or cutting, the engineers' usual rule is to prefer the latter for any depth less than sixty feet; after which it is generally cheaper to tunnel.

It does seem incongruous that William Hammond, the instigator of the railway and director of the company, would insist that a tunnel was built. According to the contemporary Encyclopaedia Britannica, railway tunnels varied from about £20 per yard in sandstone rock (which is easy to excavate and able to stand up without any lining of brickwork or masonry) - to £140 per yard in very loose ground. Ravenscar, it would appear is a fully lined top down 279 yard long 'cut and cover' tunnel. It certainly cost more than the rumoured £500. Ironically, having overcome some of the most severe engineering challenges, this unnecessary tunnel became the defining and unresolved hurdle on this stretch of railway. Tunnels on steep gradients present problems for air-breathing locomotives as the poor ventilation in the narrow tunnel starved the locomotives of power. Moisture from exhausts, natural springs and the Ravenscar sea frets combined to make the rails slippery. The gradients on this line limited the load that the locomotive could haul.

For example, on a 1% gradient (1 in 100) a locomotive can pull half, (or less) of the load that it can pull on level track. The southbound climb up to Ravenscar was 2.5% gradient (1 in 39) over three miles. The train would be literally crawling into the tunnel, out of steam. To compound this situation, it had to negotiate a curve and it is harder for a train to pull around a curve than it is on straight track. Many trains just ground to a halt, stuck in the tunnel! Even a pulley system was trialled.

In 1907, at significant cost, ten specifically designed new locomotives were purchased for this stretch of railway in an attempt to overcome the obstacles of the gradient and the tunnel. The new trains never really resolved the problem. In most picture postcards of the time, up until the introduction of diesels in the 1950s, you will see two engines chugging up the hill, one pulling from the front and one pushing from the back.

Reports from the 1930s suggest that plans were formulated to open out the tunnel due to the number of southbound trains that came to a halt in the darkness, having failed to overcome the steep gradient. Demonstrably those plans were not progressed.

From the outset, the Scarborough & Whitby Railway company line was worked by the North-Eastern Railway, but this didn't prove satisfactory and three years after it had opened the Scarborough & Whitby Railway company took the operating company, North-Eastern Railway, to court claiming that they were failing to operate the line in a profitable manner and quoting many different grievances.

The Scarborough to Whitby line was not a profitable line, partly due to the antagonism that existed between the two companies, but principally because of the vast amount of capital that had been expended. Unfortunately, by the time the line opened William Hammond was approaching death and being nursed at his London home. He did not see his railway dream come to fruition, he died at his house in Highbury, London aged 83, 3 months after the line had opened. He and his wife had produced 17 children, 8 had unfortunately failed to reach maturity. He is buried in Highgate cemetery not far from the grave of Carl Marx. His will was disputed by his family, but in the end the estate descended to four of his daughters after his wife's death in 1895. Two of his son in laws, Arthur Marshall (Chairman of the SWRC) and William Henry Bates acted as trustees of his will. Peak had mainly been used as a summer residence for the Hammond family, however he had invested much into the village. He had brought the railway, built school, a church and a mill. Did he have the first vision of Peak as a thriving holiday resort, considering that he devoted much of his life to bring the railway there?

Whatever his intentions his daughters and their husbands did not waste any time. They immediately (the same year) set about disposing of the whole estate in lots to be sold at auction. Elaborate brochures and maps were produced. However, before the auction place a private sale was struck between the trustees and two gentlemen from London: Charles Edmund Newton-Robinson and George Petter.

On the 6th of March 1895 Peak station as it was then, was closed, trains passed straight through and it was struck off the timetable. This was in retaliation by the NER that the SWRC had still not developed a waiting room at the station. For the Ravenscar plan to work it was imperative that the station, which at that time was a single platform with no facilities, needed to be reopened.

Subsequently, the Peak Estate Company signed an agreement with the SWRC on the 4th May 1896 to enable the station to open to passengers.

In a detailed agreement, the Estate Company sold a plot of land to the Railway Company for £20 to enable them to build a station master's house, which still exists. The Estate Company had to pay £50 to the Railway Company to build a ladies' waiting room and toilet on the station. Passenger services resumed on 1st April 1897.

Agreement made the fourth day of May One thousand eight hundred and ninety six **Between** The Scarborough and Whitby Railway Company hereinafter called "the Railway Company" of the one part and The Peak Estate Limited hereinafter called "the Estate Company" of the other part **Whereas** the Railway Station at the Peak on the Railway Company's line has been for some time closed **And whereas** the Estate Company are the owners of the Estate known as the Peak Estate adjoining the said Railway Station and are desirous that the said Railway Station should be reopened **And whereas** the Railway Company have agreed to reopen the said Railway Station for Passenger traffic upon the Estate Company entering into an Agreement upon the terms and conditions hereinafter contained **Now these Presents witness** that it is hereby mutually agreed as follows:—

1.— The Railway Company will open the said Railway Station upon and from the first day of April next for the purposes of Passenger traffic upon the Railway Company's line.

2.— The Estate Company will immediately provide and convey to the Railway Company the site or parcel of land for a garden and the erection of a House for the use of the Station Master of the said Station which is delineated and colored blue upon the Plan hereto annexed the Railway Company paying to the Estate Company for the provision of such site the sum of Twenty pounds.

3.— The Estate Company will at their own expense as soon as required by the Railway Company provide and maintain so long as the said Railway Station shall remain open for traffic a good and sufficient and continual supply of water to the said Station Master's house and outbuildings and to the station buildings but not for watering engines the Railway Company paying to the Estate Company therefor the yearly sum of One pound.

4.— The Estate Company at their own expense will as soon as required by the Railway Company provide proper drainage for surface water from the said Station and Station Master's House and outbuildings and will permit the Railway Company to use the said drainage free of charge

RAVENSCAR

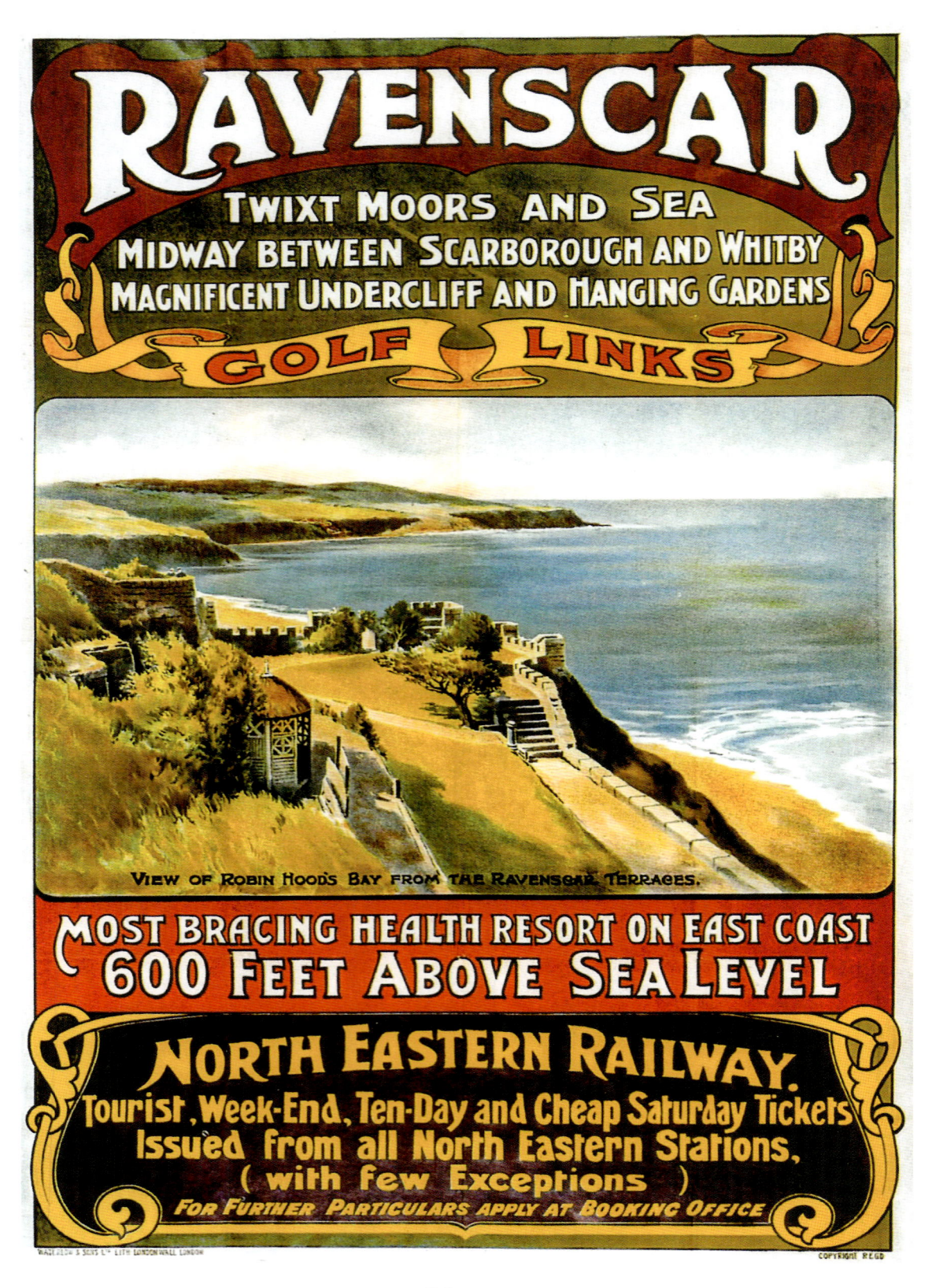

TWIXT MOORS AND SEA
MIDWAY BETWEEN SCARBOROUGH AND WHITBY
MAGNIFICENT UNDERCLIFF AND HANGING GARDENS

GOLF LINKS

View of Robin Hood's Bay from the Ravenscar Terraces.

MOST BRACING HEALTH RESORT ON EAST COAST
600 FEET ABOVE SEA LEVEL

NORTH EASTERN RAILWAY.
Tourist, Week-End, Ten-Day and Cheap Saturday Tickets Issued from all North Eastern Stations, (with few Exceptions)
For Further Particulars Apply at Booking Office

No one departs, no one arrives

Services continued for a further 68 years. As a consequence of the 'Reshaping of the Railways' report compiled by Dr Beeching, the last passenger train ran from Scarborough to Whitby on the evening of the 6th of March 1965.

Many commentators have explored the question of whether Dr Richard Beeching was little more than Genghis Khan with a slide rule, ruthlessly hacking away at Britain's rail network in a misguided quest for profitability. Or perhaps he was the fall guy for short-sighted government policies that favoured the car over the train? Recalling the halcyon days of train travel celebrated by John Betjeman and investigating the fallout of Beeching's plan, one may discover the loss to the British landscape, communities and ways of life when the railway map shrank. Knowing the difficulties our transport system is now faced with, it would seem that Beeching's plan was the biggest folly of the 1960s!

The Reshaping of the Railways report, (The Beeching Report) of 1963 dealt a hammer blow to British Railways. The government of the day welcomed the report; it saw roads as the way forward, and British Railways as a shambolic, financially incompetent drain on the state's purse. Protests resulted in the saving of some stations and lines, but the majority were closed as planned and Beeching's name remains associated with the mass closure of railways and the loss of many local services in the period that followed. A few of these routes have since reopened, some short sections have been preserved as Heritage Railways, while others been incorporated into the National Cycle Network or used for road schemes. Others are now lost to construction, simply reverted to farm land, or remain derelict. The old line between Scarborough and Whitby, passing through Ravenscar, is now known as the very popular 'Cinder Track'.

Ravenscar Station Circa 1900

Newton Robinson.   T. A. Cook.   E. Seligman.
  Sir Cosmo Duff Gordon.   Lord Desborough.

GREAT BRITAIN'S FENCING TEAM.

Copyright Photo by Bowden Bros., London.

1895

ALL CHANGE AT PEAK

Charles Edmund NewtonRobinson, (CENR) 1853-1913, was the man behind the place we all know as the 'Town That Never Was', Ravenscar. Newton was his mother's maiden name and he added it to distinguish himself from his father, Sir John Charles Robinson. He was educated at Westminster School and then at Trinity College, Cambridge and he trained and practised as a barrister having been called to the Bar in 1879.

He had many achievements to his name. He founded and chaired the Land Union, in the interest of landowners. He was a keen yachtsman, designing and building small racing yachts and he won many sailing accolades. However, it was fencing he was best known for, not only in England, but also on the Continent. He studied épée fencing in Paris in the 1890s and founded the Epée Club of London, also winning a silver medal at the 1906 Olympic games in Athens. Charles also found the time to write several volumes of poetry and was published a number of times.

CENR completed his last volume of poetry entitled Moods and Meters which was published posthumously, ending with the poem, A Tyrol Valley.

"A Tyrol Valley"

Deep would I draw one breath of Yorkshire free.
Half sea whiff and half moorland heather, now
from leagues of purple on that misty brow
where Ravenscar Juts out into the sea!
and dear are Dorset's windy downs to me
Where the white cliffs of Swanage. Like a prow,
Stem the unsleeping surge
and there below
Shelter the cosy Townlet under lee.

Gentlemen's Clubs

Many of those involved in the history of Ravenscar would have been members of gentlemen's clubs in London such as the Athenaeum, Boodles and Whites. This was considered a respectable part of the 'Establishment' at the time. By the late 19th century, any man with a credible claim to the status of 'gentleman' was eventually able to find a club willing to admit him. In these clubs, connections were made, opportunities were presented, and deals were struck. This is where the idea for another new development to create a seaside resort would have been discussed. CENR was a member of the Burlington Fine Arts Club and the Savile Club.

Iceberg Ahead

CENR's closest friend, advisor and immediate neighbour at his London address was Sir Cosmo Duff Gordon, (below) a fencing team mate at the Olympic games and a prominent Scottish landowner. Unfortunately, Duff Gordon was best known for the circumstances in which he survived the sinking of the RMS Titanic in 1912, along with his wife. They were among only 12 people who escaped in Lifeboat #1, which had a capacity of 40.

Criticism after the disaster claimed that Sir Cosmo boarded the lifeboat in violation of the "women and children first" policy and that, once the craft was afloat, he bribed its crew not to return to rescue people struggling in the water. Despite the official vindication by the Board of Trade inquiry, public suspicion that the Duff-Gordons had acted selfishly tainted the couple for the remainder of their lives.

Perhaps one of the most evocative images (below) of the Titanic disaster is that of the young newsboy outside the White Star Line offices at Oceanic House in Cockspur Street, London, S.W., holding an Evening News poster announcing, "Titanic Disaster Great Loss of Life". That boy was Ned Parfett and his short life was no less spectacular, and his death just as tragic, as that of Titanic. Six and a half years after this poignant photograph was taken, Ned was killed during a German bombardment while serving with the British army in France, just days before the Armistice. He was 22.

Sir John Charles Robinson

The plan for Ravenscar was not a new concept, it came from Charles' father, Sir John Charles Robinson. Sir John Robinson was the first superintendent of art collections at the South Kensington Museum which later became the Victoria and Albert Museum. He was considered to be one of the greatest connoisseurs and collectors of the Victorian period.

His position allowed him to travel around the world purchasing works for the museum and because of his work, it now houses the world's foremost collection of renaissance art and sculptures. He was also an art and sculpture dealer on a private basis, which was convenient given the nature of his paid job.

In 1869 he resigned his post because of a dispute with the museum. Whilst employed by the museum he had amassed a fine collection for himself during his working travels. It was by these means that he acquired himself a considerable personal fortune, rather than through the sale of his own work.

From 1882 to 1901 he became the Crown surveyor of pictures to Queen Victoria. The family now circulated in the highest levels of government and royalty.

Sir John had laid the blueprint for the seaside holiday resort schemes with successful developments in Swanage in 1872, and Lee-on-the-Solent in 1883.

Queen Victoria

CENR formed 'The Lands Trading Company' in 1884 to emulate his father's success in developing seaside resorts. The Company offices were in Chancery Lane, London.
The Company's activities consisted mainly of the purchase of moderately sized freehold estates, freehold mortgages and ground rents and the development of land and resale in lots. The Lands Trading Company would buy up estates then sell the estate to a newly formed local development specific company, usually with the same directors. The land would then be divided up into individual building plots which would be sold at public auctions. They would commence preparatory works in laying drains and basic sewer connections. Elaborate sales brochures and maps were created.

The marketing and promotion were very effective in establishing interest and early sales. Another main enticement to buy a plot at auction was the fact that you only had to pay an initial deposit and the remainder could be paid in instalments.
The Lands Trading Company directors were notable gentlemen and barristers at law; Charles Edmund Newton-Robinson, Reginald J. Lake, W. Shillito, G.M.R Layton and G.A. Petter. CENR had already commenced two similar schemes prior to Ravenscar. The first was the Tankerton Estate in Kent of 300 acres including Tankerton Castle, which came to the market in 1890.

The resemblances between Tankerton and Ravenscar, historically and geographically, are as remarkable as, surely, they are coincidental. In 1780, Tankerton was the site of a major alum works in the hands of a wealthy benefactor and landowner, Charles Pearson. He instigated the building of a railway fraught with difficulties and delays but unfortunately he died just prior to its completion. Eerily, almost identical circumstances to William Hammond, the Ravenscar philanthropist.

The Lands Trading Company purchased the Tankerton Estate in July 1890. On the 13th August 1890, they subsequently formed, incorporated and opened a bank account for The Tankerton Estate Company. By 1893 they were into their twenty-third sale and plots were selling well. In 1894, eighty-eight acres in Salcombe came to the market. Newton-Robinson had the same group of directors behind him as well as some new investors and shareholders. The same method of operation was put in place. The Lands Trading Company purchased the land and they then formed the South Devon Lands Company to sell the plots of land. On the 1st September 1894 the first sale selling the plots was up and running. This scheme proved very popular and lucrative both for the two companies and for the individuals involved.
One of those individual directors, Hugh Oakley Arnold-Forster, MP for West Belfast, was tempted in as an investor and subsequently used to help to promote the scheme. H.O. was an eminent British politician and writer. He notably served as Secretary of State for War in Arthur Balfour's Conservative government from 1903 until December 1905, as well as being a member of the Privy Council. H.O. was married to Mary, the great-granddaughter of the astronomer royal Nevil Maskelyne, whose family would subsequently have an involvement in Ravenscar.

In a time when there were no committees overseeing standards in public life or scrutiny of members' interests, MPs could openly promote their involvement in private schemes without any questions being asked of them. The morality of utilising your public position to promote and endorse private schemes was somewhat blurred. A well respected, liked and renowned politician, destined for high office, had no trouble persuading a room full of potential investors and buyers.

(Of Hugh Oakley Arnold-Forster) 'His speeches in Parliament were models of lucid exposition. He spoke, as he wrote, easily, fluently, and with an orderly evolution of his topics. He made no use of rhetorical ornament, but he seldom wearied his hearers, and never confused them by any slovenliness of preparation or obscurity of expression'.
No doubt then he was convincing. He and some of his family were to become directors and investors in the Ravenscar scheme.

Salcombe was a complete success and all of the available lots were eventually sold. Many roads in the Newton-Robinson family developments were named after directors of the company, as well as some tongue in cheek, for instance, in Salcombe 'Bonaventure Road'. In every development, with the notable exception of Ravenscar, you will find a Newton Road or Place.

Tankerton circa 1900

THE KING AND HIS NAVY AND ARMY.] [OCTOBER 17th, 1903.

With Supplement—OUR LIGHTHOUSES.

THE KING
AND HIS
NAVY & ARMY

Vol. XVII. No. 350.   SATURDAY, OCTOBER 17th, 1903.   PRICE 6D.

Elliott & Fry

The New Secretary of State for War.
Mr. H. O. Arnold-Forster, M.P.
Who was previously the Secretary to the Admiralty.

1896

BUILD IT AND THEY WILL COME

Everything seemed set fair when CENR came across the Peak Estate in 1895, encouraged by the success he was experiencing in Salcombe, and recognising a new opportunity, he set about his next plan. Maybe CNER was influenced by his wife, Janetta Anna Stirke, who was originally from Yorkshire.

Having identified the opportunity for his next scheme, on the 30th October 1895 CENR bought by private contract what had been listed in the original auction as Lots:1,2,3,4,7,8,9,10,13, for the sum of £13,000, paying a £650 deposit on the day.
On the 8th November George Petter, another business associate, who always acted as company secretary in CNER schemes, bought lots 5 & 6 for £450. Between them they had purchased over seven hundred and forty acres for £13,450.00. They chose not to buy the remaining 60 acres offered for sale originally, probably because they were outside the main Peak area.

CENR set to work establishing and formalising the structure and finance of the new project. On 19th December 1895, his own company, the Lands Trading Company, bought his private purchase of the land and buildings at Peak, together with George Petter's two lots for £15,000 (£1550 profit). On the 21st December the LTC sold the land and buildings to the newly formed Peak Estate company for £37,000 which was made of a cash payment of £17,000 and £20,000 in the form of 2,000 shares in the PEC (another £2,000 profit plus two thousand shares!). This meant that CENR and George Petter had recouped all of their original outlay, made £3550 profit and also owned half of the newly formed Peak Estate Company.

Company seal of The Peak Estate Limited

Plan of THE RAVEN HALL ESTATE PEAK YORKSHIRE.

For Sale by
MESSRS. DEBENHAM, TEWSON, FARMER & BRIDGEWATER,
Surveyors, Land Agents & Auctioneers,
80, CHEAPSIDE, LONDON, E.C.

The Raven Hall Estate, Yorkshire.

PART OF THE TERRACES.

SOLICITORS,

WILLIAM CULROSS ESQ^{RE}
9, MINCING LANE, LONDON, E.C.

MESS^{RS} TURNBULL & MOODY,
33, S^T THOMAS STREET,
SCARBOROUGH.

MESS^{RS} DEBENHAM, TEWSON, FARMER AND BRIDGEWATER,
SURVEYORS, LAND AGENTS & AUCTIONEERS
80, CHEAPSIDE,
LONDON, E.C.

C.F. KELL, LITHO 8, FURNIVAL ST HOLBORN, E.C.

KEY PLAN.

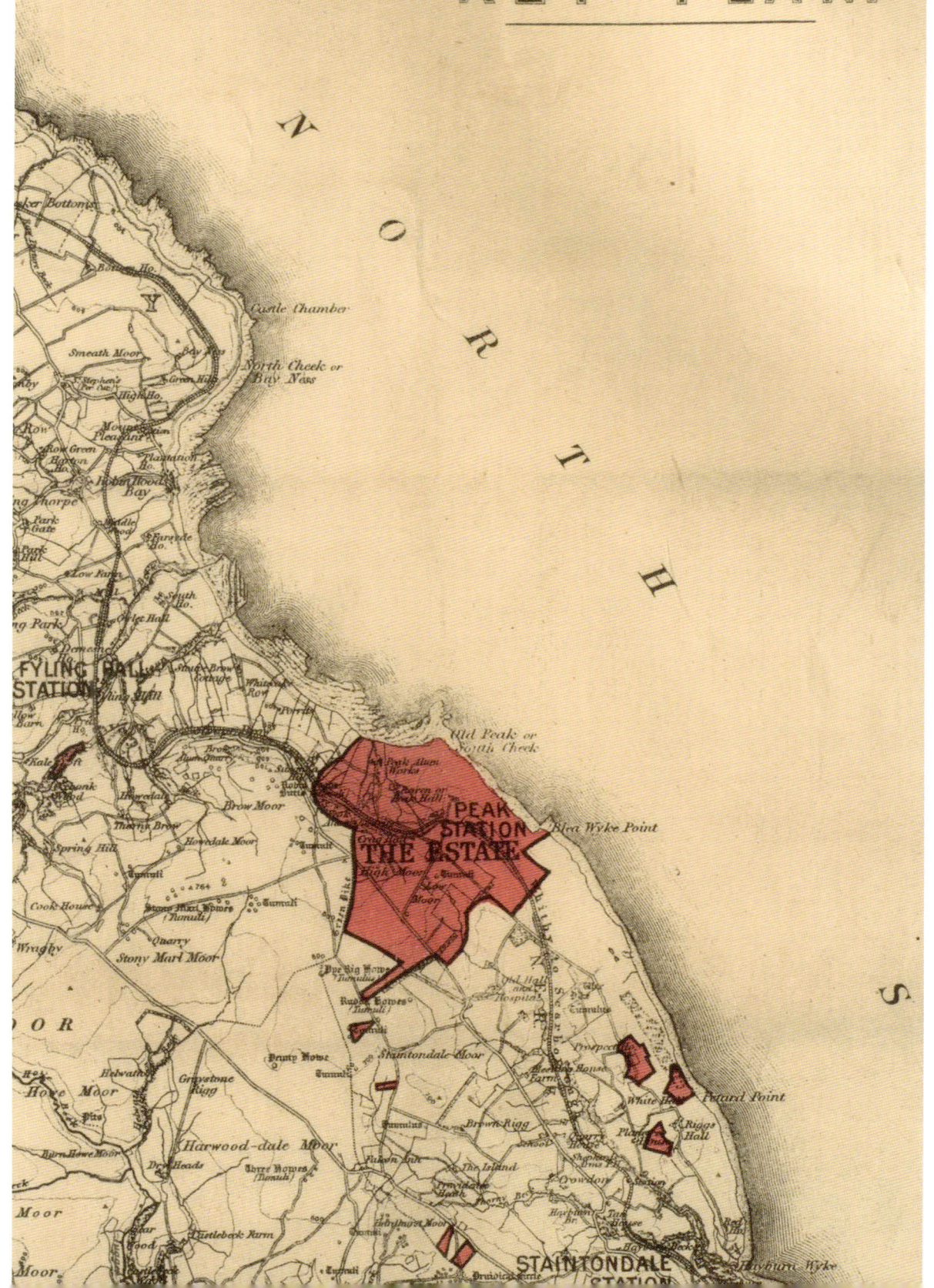

SECOND EDITION.

By Order of the Trustees of the late W. H. HAMMOND, Esq.

THE RAVEN HALL ESTATE,
PEAK, YORKSHIRE.

Occupying a grand situation amidst magnificent scenery, and bounded by sea and moor. Peak Station (at present disused) is on the Estate, and Fyling Hall, and Staintondale Stations are within about two and three miles, thus affording quick and easy access to the fashionable watering places of Scarborough and Whitby, which are distant by road about twelve and eight miles respectively.

The Particulars, Plans & Conditions of Sale
OF THE WELL-KNOWN CHOICE

FREEHOLD DOMAIN
IN THE PARISHES OF

STAINTONDALE, FYLINGDALES, AND CLOUGHTON,
Including a very substantially-built

FAMILY MANSION

In a most lovely situation on the summit of the Peak overlooking Robin Hoods' Bay, together with grounds and

Magnificent Castellated Terrace,

Well known for its singular beauty, with one end arranged as an **old Castle keep**, and commanding the most splendid and

UNSURPASSED SEA VIEWS,

The total area of the Estate is about

803a. 1r. 31p.,

LAND TAX REDEEMED AND TITHE FREE

(With the exception of a very small portion on which tithe is payable), and is divided into numerous convenient Farms, with excellent stone-built Farm Houses, Homesteads and Cottages, Residences, Inn, &c. Also

VALUABLE MINERALS, STONE QUARRIES, & MANORIAL RIGHTS.

FOR SALE BY AUCTION, BY

Messrs.
DEBENHAM, TEWSON, FARMER & BRIDGEWATER,

At the Balmoral Hotel, Scarborough,

On THURSDAY, AUGUST 15th, 1895,

At TWO for THREE o'clock precisely. In **17 LOTS.**

Particulars, with Plans, and Conditions of Sale, may be obtained of W. CULROSS, Esq., Solicitor, 9, Mincing Lane, E.C., of Messrs. TURNBULL, & MOODY, Solicitors, Scarborough; and of

THE AUCTIONEERS, 80, CHEAPSIDE, LONDON, E.C.

BRIEF ADVERTISEMENTS OF ALL PROPERTIES TO BE INCLUDED IN MESSRS. DEBENHAM, TEWSON, FARMER & BRIDGEWATER'S WEEKLY AUCTION SALES APPEAR IN "THE TIMES" EVERY SATURDAY.

LOT ONE—*continued.*

And contains the following accommodation:—

ON THE TOP FLOOR:

Billiard Room (about 25ft. 6in. by 18ft. 6in.), lighted by lanthorn light (now used as two Servants' Bed Rooms), other **Three Servants' Bed Rooms, Housemaid's Closet** with pump and copper for heating water for the bath, large Box Room in the roof, and **Soft Water Tanks** capable of holding about 1,500 gallons.

ON THE FIRST FLOOR,

Which is approached by a handsome Staircase with statue niches in the walls, **Seven Bed Rooms** measuring respectively about 21ft. by 18ft., 20ft. by 16ft. 8in., 20ft. 4in. in largest part by 13ft. 4in., 19ft. 6in. by 12 ft. 4in., 18ft. by 12ft., 12ft. 6in. by 12ft., and 12ft. 9in. by 8ft.), Bath Room, Linen Closet, and w.c. There is also a Secondary Staircase. **Elegant Drawing Room** (about 27ft. by 23ft.) with handsome marble mantel, and bay window commanding a magnificent sea view.

ON THE GROUND FLOOR:

Large **Entrance Hall** with **Portico** and long **Corridor** leading to the garden entrance.

FOUR HANDSOME RECEPTION ROOMS

Commanding magnificent views over Robin Hoods Bay, fitted with marble mantels and plate glass windows and comprising **Dining Room** (about 27ft. by 23ft.), **Morning Room** (about 20ft. by 16ft. 8in.), each with large Semi-Circular Bay, **Library** (about 19ft. 6in. by 12ft. 4in.), **Study** (about 12ft. 6in. by 12ft.), Store Room and w.c.

THE DOMESTIC OFFICES

Are well arranged on the opposite side of the Corridor and are completely shut off. They include Servants' Hall (about 20ft. 4in. by 13ft. 4in.), Large Kitchen (about 21ft. by 18ft.) with range, dresser and shelves, Back Kitchen with kitchener, sink, &c., Cook's Larder, and Butler's Pantry with sink, dresser and cupboards.

Good Vaulted Cellars in the Basement including Wine Cellar, Dairy and Summer Larder.

THE OUTBUILDINGS

Are stone built and include Lamp Room, Coal House and Servants' w.c., Cow House, Piggery, Carpenter's Shop, Cart Shed, Three Poultry Houses, and Dogs' Kennels.

THE STABLING

Comprises Two Stalls and Loose Box, Large Loft, Harness Room and

CAPITAL COACH HOUSE

For Four Carriages with two pair of entrance doors.

The roofs of the Stables and Coach House have recently been entirely re-slated and the roof of the Hall repaired, partly re-slated and re-leaded.

LOT ONE—*continued.*

At the extremity of

The Pleasure Grounds

And forming a special feature of the property is

A MAGNIFICENT TERRACE

With fine castellated wall of great length, and extending to the very edge of the beautiful gorse clad and majestic cliff, where (overlooking the Sea, some 600 feet below) it is arranged as

AN OLD CASTLE KEEP

With Battlements and Bastions, Stone Terraces, Seats, &c. These Terraces, which are well known for their singular beauty, command the most splendid and

UNSURPASSED SEA VIEWS.

Gravel Walks are laid out with Flower Borders and Shrubs and a

Level Lawn with Rustic Summer House.

THERE ARE

CHARMING TERRACED WALKS ON THE CLIFF SIDE

(And though now overgrown could readily be re-established) and the lovely Coast Scenery with the Immense Cliffs and Rocks rising in magnificent grandeur around, the beautiful sea breezes, and numerous shipping passing in the distance make this

A most Delightful and Refreshing Retreat.

There is a good

KITCHEN GARDEN

With Lean-to Greenhouse about 30ft. long, also

Two Paddocks and Orchard.

THE LANDS IN HAND

Including the Mansion and Grounds are set forth in the following SCHEDULE.

Ordnance No.	Description.	Quantity.		
		A.	R.	P.
PARISH OF STAINTONDALE.				
Pt. 493A	Selly Coom Cliff	5	0	30
496	Kitchen Garden	0	1	19
497	Pasture	0	2	16
Pt. 499	Mansion, Buildings, &c.	1	0	25
500	Pasture	3	0	4
501	Terrace	0	1	23
502	Pasture	1	0	37
503	Plantation	0	1	15
510	Rough Pasture and Wood	4	2	34
512	Ditto	4	2	16
513	Moor and Quarry	14	0	6
523	Wood	4	2	29
529	Terrace	0	2	13
PARISH OF FYLINGDALES.				
469	Rough Pasture	0	2	31
474	Alum Mine, &c.	19	1	38
	Total A.	61	0	16

THE AGREEMENT REFERRED TO IN THE WITHIN CONDITIONS OF SALE.

We, Arthur Marshall and William Henry Bates (hereinafter called the Vendors) and Charles Newton Robinson of 18 Kensington Square, London, W. (hereinafter called the Purchaser) hereby respectively declare and agree as follows:—That the Purchaser ~~was the highest bidder for and was declared~~ has purchased by private contract ~~the Purchaser of~~ the Property described as Lot 1,2,3,4,7,8,9,10 and 13, in the within Particulars, according to the within Conditions of Sale at the price of Thirteen Thousand —————— pounds and that the Purchaser has paid the sum of Six hundred and fifty —— pounds in part payment of the purchase-money to the Auctioneers, to be held by them as a deposit. And the Purchaser hereby agrees to pay the balance of the purchase-money, and the Vendors and Purchaser respectively agree to complete the said sale and purchase in all respects according to the aforesaid Conditions of Sale so far as the same are applicable to a sale by private contract

Dated this 30 day of October 1895.

Purchase-money......£ 13,000
Deposit ....£ 650
Balance ....£ 12,350

Debenham & Co.
Vendors' Agents.

Purchaser.

Abstract of Title to be sent to

Messrs Harrison & Robinson
Solrs.
762 Strand.

They immediately issued the Company prospectus, detailing the financial projections and potential returns in order to invite potential investors to raise the share capital needed. A total of four thousand shares were issued at £10 per share. Two thousand ordinary shares had already been issued as part of the purchase from the LTC. Four hundred and twenty-nine shares had already been subscribed to by the directors, their families and friends. Five hundred ordinary shares were held in reserve. This released one thousand and seventy-one shares onto the market. Seven hundred and eighty-one subscriptions were taken up. From a financial return point of view, for the plan to work for the investors, all thirteen hundred available plots had to sell for an average price of £77.

In February 1896, the Peak Estate Company commenced work laying the basic infrastructure of roads, sewers, water supply and drainage. Everything was now in place to start the promotion and marketing of the new scheme. Beautifully designed and printed sales journals and maps were produced to attract potential buyers to the auctions. These gave a very detailed description of the plots laid out before the potential purchaser; a fantastic opportunity to build and live in the most magnificent surroundings.
In October 1897 the Peak Estate Company changed its name to the Ravenscar Estate Company. Peak became known as Ravenscar.

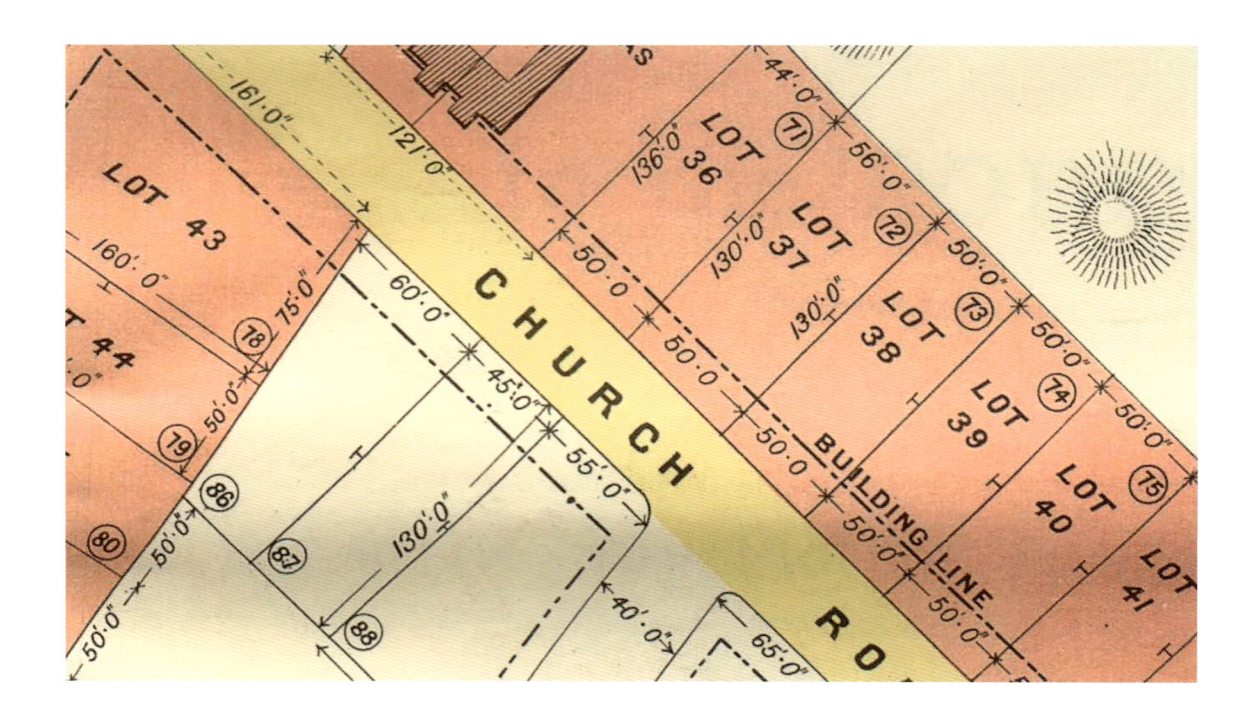

For private circulation only.

THE PEAK ESTATE
LIMITED

INCORPORATED UNDER THE COMPANIES ACTS 1862 TO 1890

Share Capital authorized - - - £40,000

In 4000 Shares of £10 each, of which 2000 are Preferred Shares entitled to a cumulative Preferential Dividend of 7 per cent. per annum (with one-half of all surplus profits after a 5 per cent. dividend has been cumulatively paid on the Ordinary Shares), and to priority in repayment of capital. The remaining 2000 are Ordinary Shares, entitled cumulatively to dividends up to 5 per cent. per annum after the Preferred Shares have received 7 per cent., and to one-half of the surplus profits thereafter.

The whole of the Ordinary Shares will be taken by the Vendors in part payment of the purchase-money of the Estate.

1071 of the Preferred Shares of £10 each are now offered for Subscription, 429 having been subscribed by the Directors and their friends before the issue of this prospectus, and the remaining 500 being held in reserve. £1 per Share is payable on application and the balance on allotment, unless the Company and the Subscriber otherwise agree.

Directors.

EDWARD BOND, Esq., M.P.
H. O. ARNOLD-FORSTER, Esq., M.P.
WILLIAM SHILLITO, Esq.
WYNDHAM R. DUNSTAN, Esq., F.R.S.
ARTHUR H. LORING, Esq.
REGINALD J. LAKE, Esq.

Bankers

Messrs. HOARE, 37, Fleet Street, London, E.C.

Solicitor.

Mr. C. E. HARRISON.

Secretary and Offices (*pro tem.*)

CHARLES CHALLIS, Esq., Clement's Inn Chambers, 263, Strand, London, W.C.

PROSPECTUS

THIS Company has been formed with the object of acquiring and developing as a new Seaside Watering Place, the valuable freehold lands known as the Peak Estate,

Robin Hood's Bay, situated about half-way between Whitby and Scarborough, amid the most magnificent cliff scenery on the Yorkshire coast.

An opportunity is now afforded of purchasing this very important freehold domain, 743 acres in extent, free of tithe and land tax, together with the mansion of Raven Hall and many other buildings thereon, and all the quarries and minerals, at the low price of £37,000, which is at the rate of less than £50 per acre. Only £17,000 of the purchase money is required to be paid in cash, as £20,000 will be taken by the vendors in Ordinary Shares.

The Peak Station of the Scarborough and Whitby Railway is upon the Estate. This line is worked by the North Eastern Railway, and the vendors have received assurances of the willingness of both Companies to re-open the station for traffic.

View of Robin Hood's Bay from the Grounds of Raven Hall.

The more valuable building lands lie near the station, at an altitude of about 600 feet above sea-level, adjacent to breezy moors, and commanding views extending southwards to Scarborough Castle and Flamborough Head. Another part of the Estate inclines with bold undulations to the beach of the well-known Robin Hood's Bay. The entire sea-front is over 7000 feet in length, and for nearly a mile it is bordered with stupendous crags, overlooking a picturesque and romantic undercliff, richly coloured with luxuriant vegetation.

In a lofty and open position stands the mansion of Raven Hall. Its site is of great interest to antiquaries, having been formerly occupied by a Roman fortress, erected (according to the inscription on the foundation-stone, now in Whitby Museum) by one Vindicianus, in the reign of the Emperor Constantine.

Surrounding the Hall are well-kept grounds, flanked by a massive turreted and crenelated rampart of stone, from whence is obtained the splendid view over Robin Hood's Bay, which is figured in the annexed illustration. The Hall is suitable for conversion into a good family hotel.

The property also comprises a well-built church, with schoolroom attached, three small villa-residences, the Raven Hill Inn, a shop and post-office, five farm-houses with outbuildings, and several cottages. Among the minerals are alum shale, cement stone, and Whitby jet. There are also vast quarries of good building stone, and rock suitable for road-making. An interest in the Royalty of the Manor of Staintondale and the Royalty of Hazelcliff passes with the Estate.

There is an abundant water-supply from a spring and reservoirs on the moor. On another part of the property the Tan Beck runs through a pretty wooded glen to the sea.

The climate is singularly bracing and healthy, and the whole neighbourhood is one of great beauty and interest. Trout-fishing and fox-hunting are to be had. The sea-fishing is good, and there are facilities for boating and bathing. Golf-links could easily be laid out.

Of late years there has arisen a large and growing demand for building land in picturesque localities on the sea-coast, to which railways have created new and improved means of cheap transit. On many estates very similar to the Peak, large profits have been realized by auction sales of building plots, the purchase-money being made payable by instalments extending over a term of years. One private land company, working on the same lines as are proposed to be followed by the Peak Estate, Limited, has for five years regularly paid dividends of ten per cent. per annum, besides laying by a reserve fund.

It is proposed to lay out the Estate for building by the construction of a Marine Parade and other new roads, the provision of sewers, and the organisation of water-supply. A few pioneer houses and shops may be erected, but it is anticipated that as in other new seaside resorts most of the building will be done at the expense of the purchasers of land.

The Peak is already much visited in the Summer season, and is conveniently near to all the great manufacturing towns of Yorkshire and Lancashire. The population of these two counties alone is upwards of seven millions, while the densely populated Midland towns will also be within easy reach.

Residents in these places will be afforded an opportunity of acquiring freehold building plots at extremely moderate prices, with most picturesque and pleasant surroundings of moors, waterfalls, rocks, cliffs, and sea.

As the result of careful calculations based upon previous experience in similar undertakings, the following figures have been arrived at :—

	£
Assuming the development to continue for 10 years :	
By Cost of management at £500 per annum	5,000
,, Cost of 50 Auction Sales, at £200 each (including Advertising, Auctioneers' fees, printing, travelling expenses, etc.)	10,000
,, Road-making and other improvements	10,000
,, Law costs	4,000
,, Sundries	4,000
Total expenses in 10 years	£33,000

On the credit side the figures are estimated as follows :—

By sale of 500 acres of building land		£100,000
,, Buildings		6,000
,, Building sites on the remaining 243 acres		4,000
Total Receipts		£110,000
Deduct Cost of Estate	£37,000	
Expenses	33,000	
		70,000
Leaves net Profit		£40,000

which would be sufficient to pay a dividend of *Ten* per cent. per annum for 10 years on the present issue of Preferred Shares amounting to £15,000—and *Eight* per cent. on the Ordinary Shares of £20,000, also to leave a reserve or bonus after returning the capital.

Nothing is here credited for house, farm, or water rents, or sale of building stone, and minerals. These emoluments may be set off against unforeseen expenses (if any), and interest on temporary loans. There are many sources of profit accruing to the landowners from the development of a new town, which cannot at the outset be appraised at a fixed value, but will possibly add greatly to the above estimated dividends. No account is taken of the cost of curbing, paving, lighting and sewers, which it is the practice to charge to the purchasers of building land. It has been arranged to raise £12,000, part of the purchase-money, on loan, to be ultimately replaced by terminable debentures, so that about £10,000 of the present issue of shares may be available as free working capital.

The above estimates are more than confirmed by a Report dated 29th November, 1895, and made by Mr. Horace A. Alexander, C.C., Architect and Surveyor, of 72, Cannon Street, wherein he states the present value of the entire property to a purchaser for profitable building development, at £41,000 ; which is £4,000 in excess of the price at which it is offered to this Company. His estimate of the gross receipts is £122,910.

According to a Report dated 30th November, 1895, of Mr. F. G. Wheatley, the well-known Auctioneer, who has had great experience in dealing with similar seaside estates in many English counties, the 500 acres of building land alone may be expected to realize £100,000 when opened up with new roads and sold in plots by auction, upon the instalment purchase system. The above reports can be seen at the Company's offices.

Two contracts have been entered into between Charles E. Newton-Robinson and George Augustus Petter of the one part, and the Lands Trading Company, Limited, of 263, Strand, of the other part, one dated the 18th day of December, 1895, and the other the 23rd day of December, 1895.

By an Agreement dated the 21st day of December 1895, and made between the said Lands Trading Company, Limited, who are the promoters and vendors, of the one part, and the Peak Estate, Limited, of the other part, the Vendors agree to sell the property known as the Peak or Raven Hall Estate, comprising 743 acres, in fee simple, free of tithe and land-tax, with the mansion and other buildings thereon, the minerals and all appurtenances, at the price of £37,000, payable as to £17,000 in cash, and as to £20,000 in fully paid ordinary shares of the Peak Estate, Limited. The Vendors further agree (*inter alia*) to pay all the costs of promotion and registration of the Peak Estate, Limited. They stipulate for the right of subscription at par of such balance of this issue of £15,000 Preferred Shares as may remain unallotted on the 25th March, 1896. A copy of the above contract and the said agreement can be seen at the Company's offices.

If no allotment is made, or if the above mentioned draft agreement is not adopted, the deposit will be returned in full, and where the amount allotted is less than that asked for, the balance will be applied towards the payment due on allotment, and any excess will be returned to the applicant.

Application for the Preferred Shares may be made on the accompanying form, and forwarded with the amount payable on deposit either to the Company's bankers or to the Secretary at the Company's Offices.

Prospectuses and Forms of Application may be obtained from the Secretary.

London, 21*st December*, 1895.

THE
PEAK ESTATE
LIMITED

Share Capital authorized - - - £40,000

Issue of £15,000 Mortgage Debentures

(part of a series of £20,000), bearing Interest at the rate of £5 per centum per annum, and repayable in 1899, 1901, or 1903, at the option of the Subscriber.

Directors.
EDWARD BOND, Esq., M.P. (*Chairman*).
H. O. ARNOLD-FORSTER, Esq., M.P.
WILLIAM SHILLITO, Esq.
WYNDHAM R. DUNSTAN, Esq., F.R.S.
ARTHUR H. LORING, Esq.
REGINALD J. LAKE, Esq.
CHARLES E. NEWTON-ROBINSON, Esq.

Bankers.
Messrs. HOARE, 37, Fleet Street, London, E.C.

Solicitor.
C. E. HARRISON, Esq., 263, Strand, W.C.

Secretary and Offices.
G. A. PETTER, Esq., 263, Strand, London, W.C.

PROSPECTUS

THIS Company was formed with the object of acquiring and developing as a new Seaside Watering Place, to be named "Ravenscar," the valuable freehold property known as the Peak Estate, Robin Hood's Bay, situated about half-way between Whitby and Scarborough, on the Yorkshire coast. The Estate, which is 743 acres in extent and comprises the mansion of Raven Hall, a church, and about a dozen farm houses, villas and cottages, and large quarries of building stone, was acquired at the price of £37,000, of which £20,000 was taken by the vendors in fully paid-up Ordinary Shares.

The Scarborough and Whitby Railway Company, whose line is now being worked by the North Eastern Railway, has a station upon the Estate.

Since the property was acquired, a very successful auction sale of building plots has been held; the formation of roads and paths has been commenced, and the Hall is being furnished and decorated with the view of its being opened as an hotel during the present season.

The Debentures now offered for subscription constitute a floating charge on the whole undertaking of the Company, and form part of a series of £20,000, £5000 of which are reserved for issue at a later date if required. They will bear interest as from the date of the receipt of the money by the Company at the rate of £5 per centum per annum, payable on the 15th day of April and the 15th day of October, and will be for sums of £50 or any multiple thereof, as the subscriber may prefer. The principal will be repayable on the 15th of October, 1899, 1901, or 1903, at the option of the applicant. The Company reserves the right of paying off any Debenture with a premium of £2 per cent. at any time after giving two calendar months' notice.

The proceeds of this issue will be applied to the repayment of a loan of £12,000 from the Company's bankers at present secured by an equitable charge on the estate, and to the general purposes of the Company.

The form of Debenture may be inspected at the Office of the Company, 263, Strand.

29th July, 1896.

Maps that tell & maps that sell

The detailed and beautifully coloured maps of the Estate were hand-drawn in the London Drawing Office. This was the same office from which the maps were compiled for Charles Booth's inquiry into the "Life and Labour of the People in London", undertaken between 1886 and 1903.

Charles Booth was one of those remarkable English Victorians who can justifiably be described as one of the great and the good. Profoundly concerned by contemporary social problems, and not a pious nor religious man, he recognised the limitations of philanthropy and conditional charity in addressing the poverty which scarred British society. Without any commission other than his own, he devised, organised and funded one of the most comprehensive and scientific social surveys of London life that had then been undertaken thus far.

Booth also added his voice to the cause of state old age pensions as a practical instrument of social policy to alleviate destitution in old age which was established as one of the most common causes of pauperism.

The 'Maps Descriptive of London Poverty' is perhaps the most distinctive product of Charles Booth's Inquiry into Life and Labour in London (1886-1903). An early example of social cartography, each street is coloured to indicate the income and social class of its inhabitants. Simultaneously he was a successful businessman, running international interests in the leather industry and a steam shipping line. On the opposite page is one edition of the twelve Maps Descriptive of London Poverty, 1898-9 cover an area of London from Hammersmith in the west, to Greenwich in the east, and from Hampstead in the north to Clapham in the south. An early example of social cartography, each street is coloured to indicate the income and social class of its inhabitants.

Charles Booth was a promoter of the Ravenscar scheme and loaned money to the Ravenscar Estate Company in the form of a debenture for £500.

Debentures

A debenture is a long-term security yielding a fixed rate of interest, issued by a company and secured against its assets. The holder of a debenture often has the right to appoint a receiver and takes priority in recouping his money in the event of the company becoming insolvent.

MAP DESCRIPTIVE OF LONDON POVERTY, 1898-9
(IN 12 SHEETS)

SHEET 1.
EASTERN DISTRICT.

THE STREETS ARE COLOURED ACCORDING TO THE GENERAL CONDITION OF THE INHABITANTS, AS UNDER:—

Black	Dark Blue	Light Blue	Purple	Pink	Red	NIL	Yellow
Lowest class. Vicious, semi-criminal.	Very poor, casual. Chronic want.	Poor. 18s. to 21s. a week for a moderate family.	Mixed. Some comfortable, others poor.	Fairly comfortable. Good ordinary earnings.	Middle class. Well-to-do.		Upper-middle and Upper classes. Wealthy.

A combination of colours—as dark blue and black, or pink and red—indicates that the street contains a fair proportion of each of the classes represented by the respective colours.

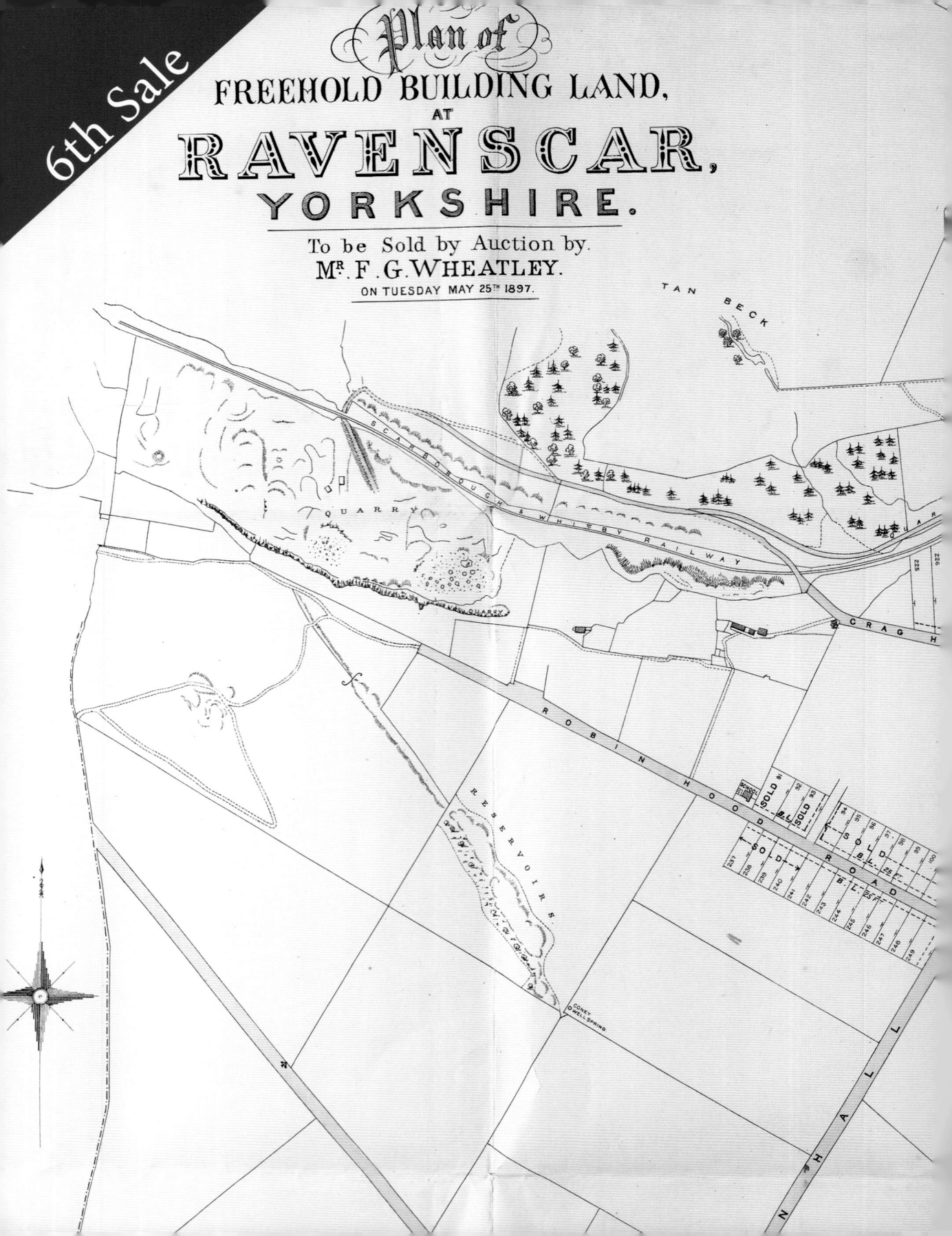

Plan of Freehold Building Land, at RAVENSCAR, YORKSHIRE.

To be Sold by Auction by
Mr. F. G. WHEATLEY.
ON TUESDAY MAY 25TH 1897.

6th Sale

THE NORTH SEA.

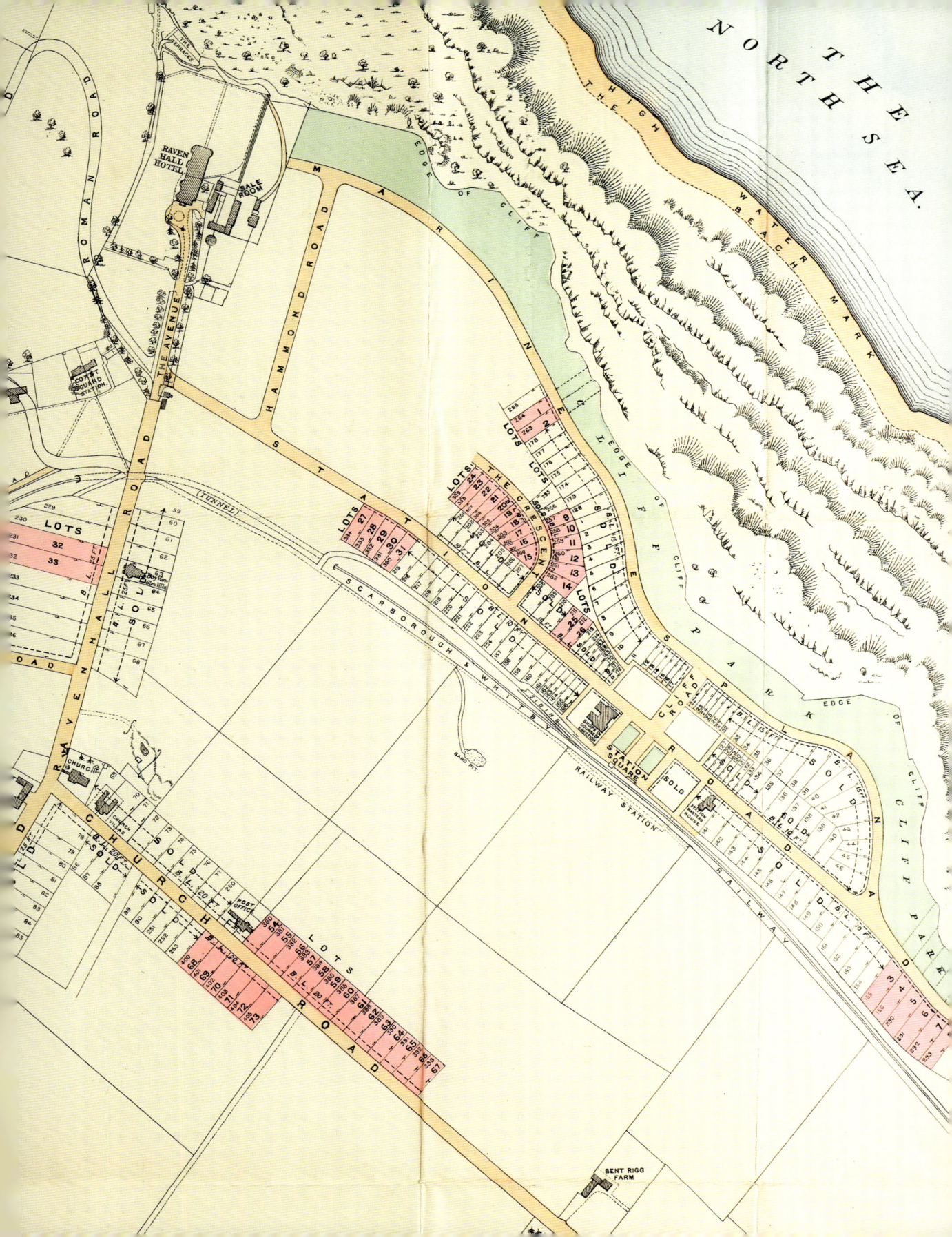

RAVEN HALL HOTEL
SALE ROOM
ROMAN ROAD
THE AVENUE
COAST GUARD STATION
HAMMOND ROAD
MARINE DRIVE
EDGE OF CLIFF
HIGH WATER BEACH MARK

TUNNEL
LOTS
LOTS: THE CRESCENT
SCARBOROUGH & WHITBY RAILWAY
STATION SQUARE
RAILWAY STATION
SAND PIT
CLIFF PARK
EDGE OF CLIFF

RAVEN HALL ROAD
CHURCH
CHURCH VILLAS
POST OFFICE
CHURCH ROAD
LOTS

BENT RIGG FARM

39th Sale

RAVENSCAR, YORKSHIRE

TO BE SOLD BY AUCTION BY
Mr ARTHUR LAWSON F.A.I. (OF YORK)
ON MONDAY, SEPTEMBER 1st 1902.

SECOND EDITION, REVISED.

FIRST AUCTION SALE.

Ten per cent. only of the Purchase-money of Building Land required to be paid down, and the balance by instalments, extending over three, five, or seven years (if desired), with interest at 5 per cent. per annum. Deeds free of law costs on acceptance of title by Purchaser. (See Conditions of Sale.)

RAVENSCAR, ROBIN HOOD'S BAY,

The New Seaside Watering-place on the Yorkshire Coast between Whitby and Scarborough. The Peak Railway Station is on the Estate.

Particulars and Conditions of Sale,

With Plans, of

77 LOTS OF FREEHOLD

BUILDING LAND

SITUATED AT RAVENSCAR, YORKSHIRE,

(SOLD FREE OF TITHE AND LAND TAX)

Amongst which are to be found

Sites for Marine Villas of every size and class,

Commanding Magnificent Views over Sea and Moors, and extending on the one hand to Robin Hood's Bay, and on the other to Scarborough Castle and Flamborough Head. The Frontages are mostly on the Marine Esplanade, the Raven Hall Road, and the main road leading from Scarborough; and the Plots lie very high on a dry, rocky subsoil, open to sunlight and bracing breezes.

ALSO THREE FREEHOLD HOUSES.

Mr. F. G. WHEATLEY

Is favoured with instructions from the Peak Estate Limited,

To Sell the above Valuable Properties by Public Auction,

In the Assembly Room at the RAVEN HALL HOTEL,

ON THE ESTATE,

On TUESDAY, JULY 7th, 1896, at 3 p.m.

Preceded by a LUNCHEON at 2 p.m. by Tickets (not transferable), to be obtained only of the Auctioneer.

1896 - 1909

PLOTS UNDER THE HAMMER

On the 7th of July 1896, 'a substantial luncheon' was held at Raven Hill Hall. This was attended by the Chairman & Directors of the PEC, notably Mr Edward Bond MP, East Nottingham, Mr HO Arnold Foster MP, West Belfast, Wyndham Dunstan FRS. (Fellowship of the Royal Society, the oldest scientific academy in continuous existence. It is a significant honour which has been awarded to many eminent scientists from history including Isaac Newton & Charles Darwin). Also having lunch along with the main shareholder CENR were the other directors, Company Secretary Thomas Wilkinson, Arthur Lorring, gentleman, Charles
Harrison, solicitor and Reginal Lake, barrister, who were joined by invited guests and registered bidders for the subsequent first auction. Great conviviality and bon viveur were enjoyed by those around the table.

An article that appeared at the same time in the Leeds Mercury newspaper, reported that at a luncheon a Mr Valentine Fowler, prominent Estate Agent and soon to be Mayor of Scarborough proposed a toast 'To the success of the Ravenscar Estate' (applause), and said he believed its success was assured, he went on to state that he thought it would be an investment no one would have cause to regret (Hear, hear).

At the first sale, seventy-seven lots were offered, and thirty-eight plots were sold. Nineteen of these plots were bought by the directors, who bid between themselves, in effect to set the market price. The plots achieved an average sale price of £66, £11 short of the investors' target. CENR continued to buy and in the first three sales in 1896, he had personally bought over 40 plots.

The sales were reported both locally and nationally in many newspapers and the potential buyers started to flood to Ravenscar.

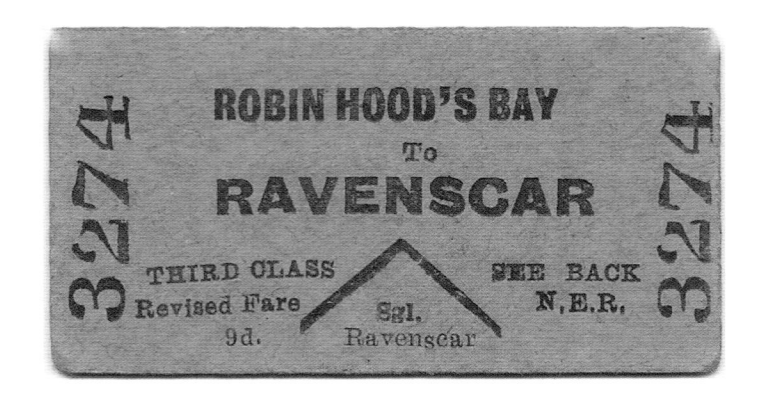

NOTE.—Special Arrangements have been made, under which intending Buyers can obtain from the Auctioneer return railway passes for Ravenscar from York at a Single Fare for the Double Journey. The train will leave York at 9-7 a.m., and Malton at 9-39 a.m., arriving at Scarborough in time for the train to Ravenscar at 10-24 a.m.

Intending Buyers from Leeds can obtain from the Secretary of the Ravenscar Estate Limited, 27, Chancery Lane, London, Return Railway Passes at a Single Fare for the Double Journey. The train leaves Leeds (North Eastern) at 8·17 a.m., arriving at York in time for the above-mentioned 9-7 a.m. train to Scarborough.

SCARBOROUGH BUYERS will join the above mentioned 10-24 a.m. train for Ravenscar.

(Passengers will return from Ravenscar at 5-10 p.m., and from Scarborough at 5-55 p.m.)

BUYERS FROM BRADFORD, LEEDS, SHEFFIELD, YORK, HARROGATE, MIDDLESBROUGH, STOCKTON, DARLINGTON, and surrounding towns, will have their train fare returned to them on becoming purchasers.

For further particulars and conditions, &c., apply to—

Mr. Arthur Lawson, Auctioneer,

12, NEW STREET,

YORK.

RAVENSCAR.

In Roman Road and The Avenue,
(Continued).

No. on Estate Plan

LOT **39**	A very valuable **Plot,** adjoining Lot 38, with frontage of 44 feet 6 inches, and depth on the northerly side of 139 feet and on the southerly side of 109 feet 6 inches. The width on the back boundary is 30 feet. Area 414 sup. square yards.	448
LOT **40**	The **Adjoining Corner Plot,** with the long frontage of 140 feet to Roman Road, and depth on the northerly side of 109 feet 6 inches. The width on the back boundary is 75 feet 6 inches. Area about 553 sup. square yards.	449
LOT **41**	An extremely valuable **Freehold Building Plot,** adjoining the grounds of the Raven Hall Hotel, and possessing the frontage of 30 feet to the Avenue, and widening to 60 feet along the building line, which is set back 51 feet 9 inches from the Avenue. The depth on the northerly side is 100 feet, and on the southerly side about 151 feet 9 inches, and the width on the back boundary is 60 feet. Area about 900 sup. square yards.	611

FROM THE BEACON.—LOOKING SOUTH.

RAVENSCAR.

In Roman Road.
(Continued.)

This new thoroughfare has opened up some charming building sites, and will probably become the main approach to the western portion of the Estate.

(The Building Line is set back 10 feet.)

Lots 42 and 43 command magnificent sea views. The Vendors will covenant with each Purchaser in the conveyances of these Lots that no building except a fence or wall not exceeding 5 feet in height shall be erected above the present level of the surface of the ground on the land in front of each Lot, and lying between plots 1036 and 1037.

Lots 42 and 43 have an accommodation road at the back.

LOT 42   A very imposing and extremely valuable parcel of **FREEHOLD BUILDING LAND,** occupying a magnificent position at the junction of Roman Road and Saxon Road. This lot has the long frontage to Roman Road of 87 feet, narrowing to 60 feet at the back, and return frontage to Saxon Road, to which the building line is set back 10 feet, of 200 feet. The area is about 1,633 sup. square yards. This lot is suitable for the erection of a first-class Villa Residence of the value of not less than £750, or a pair of semi-detached Villas costing at least £600 each.   1283

LOT 43   The **ADJOINING PLOT** with frontage of about 60 feet, and depth of 200 feet. Area about 1,333 sup. square yards. This lot will be sold subject to similar building stipulations to those applicable to Lot 42.   1284

THE ~~PEAK~~ RAVENSCAR ESTATE, LIMITED.

No. on Estate Plan.	SITUATION.	Sale.	Lot.	Purchase Money. £ s. d.	Deposit. £ s. d.	Front-age.	Depth.	Nominal Reserve. £ s. d.
64	Raven Hall Rd.	1	31	47 . .	4 14 .	55	160	60 . .
65	do.	2	38	48 . .	4 16 .	55	160	60 . .
66	do	2	39	48 . .	4 16 .	55	160	60 . .
67	do	2	40	49 . .	4 18 .	55	160	60 . .
68	do.	2	41	61 . .	6 2 .	70	160	80 . .
69	Church Road	1	35	} 517 10 .	51 15 .			600 . .
70	do	1	35					
71	do	3	38	35 10 .	3 11 .	50	136	45 . .

RAVENSCAR.

In Roman Road.
(Continued.)

LOT 16   A very imposing and extremely valuable parcel of **FREEHOLD BUILDING LAND,** occupying a magnificent position at the junction of Roman Road with Dane Road. This lot has the long frontage to Roman Road of 104 feet, narrowing to 50 feet at the back, and return frontage to Dane Road, to which the building line is set back 10 feet, of 206 feet, and depth on the easterly side of 200 feet. The area is about 1,711 sup. square yards. This lot is suitable for the erection of a first-class Villa Residence of the value of not less than £750, or a pair of semi-detached Villas costing at least £600 each.   1206

LOT 17   A very imposing and extremely valuable parcel of **FREEHOLD BUILDING LAND,** occupying a splendid position on the southerly side of Roman Road, with the long frontage of 60 feet, and the unusual depth of 200 feet. The area is about 1333 sup. square yards. This lot is also suitable for the erection of a first-class Villa Residence of the value of not less than £750, or a pair of semi-detached Villas costing at least £600 each.   1285

LOT 18   The **ADJOINING CORNER PLOT,** with frontage of about 65 feet, widening to 93 feet at the back, and return frontage to Dane Road (to which the building line is set back 10 feet). The depth is 200 feet. Area about 1,755 sup. square yards. This lot will be sold subject to similar building stipulations to those applicable to Lot 17.   1286

RAVENSCAR.

On the MARINE ESPLANADE.

The Vendors will covenant with the Purchaser in the conveyance of Lot 52 that no building except a fence or wall not exceeding 5 feet in height shall be erected above the present level of the surface of the ground on that portion of the Cliff Park in front of the Lot which is included between two parallel straight lines drawn to the edge of the Cliff in continuation of the side boundary lines of such lot, as shown by the dotted lines on the Plan.

LOT 52 A charmingly situated and well designed **Freehold Detached Villa Residence,** erected according to the plans and under the supervision of an eminent architect, and which will be sold with **vacant possession.**

The accommodation is as follows: On the Ground Floor—Vestibule and Entrance Hall, 18ft. by 12ft. 9in.; Dining Room, 14ft. 3in. by 13ft.; Drawing Room, 15ft. 3in. by 12ft. 6in.; Morning Room, 13ft. by 9ft. 6in.; Kitchen, 13ft. by 12ft. 9in.; Good Scullery, Lavatory, 2 W.C.'s; Drying Room and Coals. On the First Floor—Six Bedrooms, 13ft. 6in. by 13ft. 6in.; 16ft. 6in. by 10ft. 9in.; 12ft. by 11ft.; 15ft. 3in. by 10ft. 4in.; 13ft. 3in. by 13ft. 3in., and 15ft. 6in. by 12ft. 6in.; and on the Upper Floor—Two Bedrooms, each 17ft. by 9ft.; Bath Room, Large Store Room and Box Cupboard. The House is very substantially built and commands magnificent sea views, and is close to the Railway Station. Water is laid on from the new mains. The enclosed Garden has a frontage of 68 feet to the Marine Esplanade, to which the building line is set back 15 feet, the depth on the North-Westerly side being 99 feet, and on the South-Easterly side 96 feet. The superficial area of the site is 736 square yards.

There is an accommodation road at the back.

N.B.—The provisions of the 16th condition as to completion by instalments do not apply to Lot 52, but arrangements can, if desired, be made for payment of four-fifths of the purchase money by instalments extending over a period not exceeding ten years.

RAVENSCAR.

AT THE CORNER OF RAVEN HALL & CRAG HILL ROADS.

LOT 31 A charmingly situated and well designed **Freehold Detached Villa Residence,** erected according to the plans and under the supervision of an eminent architect, and which will be sold with **vacant possession.**

The accommodation is as follows : On the Ground Floor—Vestibule and Entrance Hall, Dining Room, 15ft. 3in. by 12ft. 9in.; Drawing Room, 15ft. 3in. by 12ft. 9in.; Kitchen, 16ft. 3in. by 13ft.; Scullery, 12ft. 9in. by 8ft. 9in.; Lavatory, 2 W.C.'s, Larder, and Coals. On the First Floor—Five Bedrooms, 17ft. by 13ft., 17ft. by 13ft., 13ft. by 12ft. 9in., 13ft. by 10ft. 6in., and 11ft. 9in. by 11ft. 9in.; and Bath Room (hot and cold); and on the Upper Floor—Nursery, 13ft. 6in. by 13ft. 3in., and Servants' Bedroom. The House is very substantially built, and of a pleasing elevation. It stands on high ground, and commands magnificent views on all sides. It is close to St. Hilda's Church, and is within a few minutes' walk of the Ravenscar Railway Station and the Raven Hall Hotel. Water is laid on from the new mains. The enclosed Garden has a frontage of 100 feet to Raven Hall Road, and a return frontage of 120 feet to Crag Hill Road, to both of which roads the building line is set back 25 feet. The superficial area of the site is 1,333 square yards.

There is an accommodation road on the westerly side.

N.B.—The provisions of the 16th condition as to completion by instalments do not apply to Lot 31, but arrangements can, if desired, be made for payment of four-fifths of the purchase money by instalments extending over a period not exceeding ten years.

Some Houses designed by . . . . .
   the Architect to this Estate, . .
   FRANK A. TUGWELL, A.R.I.B.A.,
   102, Westborough, Scarborough. .

Grand Designs

The architect commissioned by the Peak Estate Company to design the properties which would be built at Ravenscar was Frank A. Tugwell, A.R.I.B.A. His practice was based in Scarborough. Adjacent you can see examples of Tugwell's designs, many of which you can still see today in Scarborough, Filey, throughout the Moors and all along the Yorkshire coast. He was also the architect responsible for the redesign of the Victorian auditorium in the Savoy Theatre in 1929.

The Ravenscar Estate Company built four lots of properties designed by Tugwell referred to in the prospectus as 'Pioneer houses'. These were 'Corbie' on Marine Esplanade, 'New Villa' on Raven Hall Road, the four terraced villas in Loring Road as well as the shops and boarding house built in Station Square. These were built to show the range of possible building designs available within the scheme. There was something for all.

The vision of the new Yorkshire watering hole was of a residential seaside resort with large villas for wealthy Victorians. However, this would also require a local workforce to meet the needs of the new residents and to provide a full range of shops and services. The building of humbler properties for the 'workers' were destined for considerably smaller plots such as those on Stansfield Place. The idea was that the purchasers of larger plots should perhaps consider also building a property on Stansfield Place for those who serviced their wants and needs, so that it was far enough away so as to not intrude on the privacy of the residents of the villas or mansions!

Facing page bottom right picture Ramshill Hotel Scarborough
Facing page centre picture and below (today) Belvedere Road Scarborough

The brochures and the maps painted a picture of a new life and a great new opportunity. It was within the grasp of so many who aspired to a connection to Ravenscar.

Work had begun immediately on turning Raven Hill Hall into a hotel. An extension of 50 rooms was planned for the building. It was to be decorated and finished to the highest standards of the day.

At the sixth sale on the 25th of May 1897 another luncheon was held and attended by the directors and local dignitaries. When asked about the hotel, HO stated that the Company may part with the hotel and that personally he would like to retain possession, but if the pending negotiations succeeded in a sale then the result would introduce further enterprise and additional capital into the work.

By September 1897 almost £20,000 had been spent by the Ravenscar Estate Company extending and renovating Raven Hill Hall into a first-class hotel. Still in an unfinished state it was sold in October 1897 to Walter James Hudson, a wealthy hotelier from London with connections to the Berkley hotel in Knightsbridge and numerous other hotels around the country.

Walter Hudson also acquired the Crown Hotel, the Queens Hotel and the Royal Hotel in Scarborough, along with The Royal Crescent Hotel and Ackworth House in Filey, which was also to be transformed into a hotel. He subsequently sold the hotels to a new company he formed himself, 'Hudson Hotels Limited' for £240,000 in January 1898.

On the 4th of October 1897 the ledgers from Hoares Bank London confirm that the Ravenscar Estate Company repaid the outstanding balance of £8,400 of the original £12,000 loan it had taken out at the start of the scheme. At present we have no record of how much Hudson actually paid for Raven Hill Hall. The payment did not appear in the Ravenscar Estate account at Hoares Bank.

Measurement of Work executed at the Raven Hall Hotel Ravenscar Scarborough by the Peak Estate Company Limited for which the Purchaser is liable to the Vendors under the Clauses of an Agreement dated.—

September 1897.

Masonry.

			£	s	d
Feet					
20,080	Cube Winning & haulage of stone (744 cubic yards) at	5/6 per yard	204	12	0
8,241	Sup. D⁰. D⁰. and dressing of facing stones	2/1½	875	12	0
557	„ D⁰. D⁰. (circular)	2/1½	59	3	6
N⁰ 288	Loads of sand	1/9	25	4	0
N⁰ 5	Stone templates				

Rods	feet		Cwts qrs lbs			
28	179	Sup Reduced brickwork	12 Tons per Rod	7440	0	0
3 (Rods)	2347	„ Half brick walls				
	N⁰ 27	Chimney Pots 3'6" high		14	0	0

Squares	feet				
37	40	Sup Slating	262	0	0
	51	Run Terro metallic ridge tiling	5	0	0

Continued 7721 0 0   £1164 . 11 . 8

MEMORANDUM OF AGREEMENT.

I J. Maryon of 1 Eldon St Finsbury E.C. admit that I was the highest bidder for and became the purchaser of Lot 25 described in the within Particulars at the Auction Sale thereof, and I hereby agree to buy the same for the sum of £ 68 from THE PEAK ESTATE, LIMITED, of 263, Strand, London, W.C., subject to the within Particulars, Conditions, Stipulations and Plans, and have paid the sum of £ 6.16/— as a deposit on account of the said purchase-money into the hands of the Auctioneer *[and I elect to complete the purchase by equal half-yearly instalments according to the terms and conditions set forth in the Schedule herewith annexed].

Dated this 7th day of July, 1896.

Purchase-money	£ 68 : —
Deposit	£ 6 : 16 : —
Balance	£ 61 : 4 : —

John Maryon

As Auctioneer and Agent for the above-named Vendors I confirm the Sale of the above premises, and acknowledge to have received the said Deposit.

On successfully bidding on a plot, the hammer went down and the deal was struck. The buyer immediately entered into, and signed, a memorandum of agreement with the Ravenscar Estate Company in the saleroom.

As most of the directors were barristers and solicitors, they had clearly used their expertise to extensively develop general conditions of sale and subsequent building stipulations. These were onerous, explicit and legally binding. Although clearly laid out in the small print, there was much to comply with, and many penalties were liable to be charged and monies demanded if the rules were not adhered to. The purchaser was required to submit full designs and material lists to the Ravenscar Estate Company for the property they wished to erect for approval. These would be inspected for a fee of 1 guinea. The properties that were permitted to be built had to have a minimum value starting at £150 for those on Stansfield Place to £750 for those situated on Marine Esplanade. Hotel sites were to be a minimum of £2,000 in value.

The purchaser was liable for all costs of installing water supply and sewerage from the mains to their property which was charged at four shillings per foot. Buyers were also obligated that on demand by the Estate surveyor, they would have to pay towards roads and paving being installed and maintained.

As an incentive to those who could perhaps not afford to buy the plot outright, they could purchase the plot by an instalment option. At the sale they agreed to deposit ten percent of the purchase price, the remaining balance being due by two instalments annually until the balance was paid. This could be spread over a maximum of 9 years at five percent interest per annum. Should the purchaser choose to pay outright, the balance became due within 28 days. If they failed to pay or were late by 14 days with their instalments, the contract was rescinded and all costs became due. The Ravenscar Estate Company would re-auction the plot and pursue the original purchaser through the courts for costs and interest.

Let's halt a while

The extract opposite is from Ashley Courtneys famous series of travel guides 'Lets Halt a While', 1949 edition. Raven Hall Hotel still remains a most unique hotel.

Low Peak Farm
Ravenscar
Yorks.

The Hotel shown on the other side might suit you for a few days. Scenery grand overlooking R.H. Bay. Golf Links & shooting near by. easy distance of station — but there are no other attractions, very quiet — over 600 ft above sea level.

W. J. Wynn Esq.
c/o London & Westminster Bk Ld
Temple Bar
London.

Raven Hall Hotel *Tel. Cloughton 33*

A Lancashire reader asked me if I knew of an hotel in the south of England to be compared with this self-contained holiday hotel on the Yorkshire coast, and I replied " There is no other hotel in Britain comparable with Raven Hall. Some can offer some of its facilities. None can offer all." Take its position, 600 feet above sea level. An unrestricted panoramic coastal vista stretching from Robin Hood's Bay on the left to Scarborough Castle and Filey Brig on the right. Behind are hundreds of acres of moorland—a picture in the ever changing lights. In such an invigorating location youth quickly dons its sports kit and its elders cast off business and domestic care.

The Raven Hall sea water swimming bath is unique. 100 ft. by 35 ft. Sea water is pumped direct from the sea, and, passing through a filtration and chlorination plant, is sparkling clear and clean. An interesting feature, Mr. J. R. Cooper, the resident managing director, told me, was that as the season progresses the brine becomes denser and the water more buoyant, so beginners find themselves swimming almost before they realise it. Glass screens around the pool act as a wind shield and as a background for sun bathing.

Stacks of golf clubs in the hall are evidence of the popularity of Raven Hall for golfers. The hotel has a private nine-hole sporting course where, if you drive out of bounds, it means a 600 ft. drop and splosh . . . the sea! The hotel also provides hard tennis courts, putting course, bowling green, and indoors a billiards room and ballroom with regular dances, with orchestra. A resident host arranges competitions and tournaments, treasure hunts, and in other ways keeps the holiday party spirit going amongst the energy spenders. At the same time Raven Hall is large enough to cater for those who just seek rest. The sunken terraced gardens, cosy lounges and quiet bedrooms are invitations to relaxation. In short a self-contained holiday resort which caters for all ages and all tastes. *Fully licensed. From 30/- a day. B. & B. from 20/-. Meals:* L. 4/6. Tea 2/-. D. 5/-. 10% *Service charge. Garage:* 11 *lock-ups*, 3/-; 21 *cars in large garage*, 1/6. *Bedrooms:* 60 *d.*, 6 *s. Electric fires. London* 248, *Whitby* 14, *Scarborough* 10½.

By order of the Receiver for the Debenture Holders.

RAVENSCAR,
ROBIN HOOD'S BAY.

The New Seaside Watering Place on the Yorkshire Coast, midway between Scarborough and Whitby, commanding MAGNIFICENT VIEWS over Sea and Moors, and extending on the one hand to Robin Hood's Bay, and on the other to Scarborough Castle and Flamborough Head. The Estate lies very high on a dry, rocky subsoil, open to sunlight and bracing breezes. The cliffs are 600 feet high.

Ravenscar Railway Station is on the Estate.

Particulars and Conditions of Sale

——— OF ABOUT ———

225 ACRES
— OF —
FREEHOLD BUILDING LAND,

In large and small plots of varied dimensions to suit all purchasers. Beautifully situated and occuping some of the choicest positions on the Ravenscar Estate,

TO BE SOLD BY AUCTION BY
Messrs. STANLEY ATHERTON & Co.
— AT THE —
RECREATION HALL, CHURCH ROAD (on the Estate),
On WEDNESDAY, AUGUST 15th, 1923,
At 3.30 o'clock, p.m.

At VERY LOW RESERVES to CLOSE THE ESTATE.

The Estate Foreman, Mr. C. WRIGHTSON, will show the sites suitable for

Bungalows, and Houses of all descriptions, and

SMALL POULTRY FARMS,

To PROSPECTIVE BUYERS, on application at the ESTATE OFFICE, STATION SQUARE, RAVENSCAR,

---

Particulars, Plans, and Prices to be obtained of—
Secretary of the Ravenscar Estate, Limited, and Receiver for the Debenture Holders:
G. A. PETTER, ESQ., F.C.A.
(Maddox, Savage, Petter & Co.),
28, Budge Row, London, E.C.
Tel., City 5932 & 5933.

Solicitors: Messrs. PEARCE & NICHOLLS,
12, New Court,
London, W.C.

Auctioneers: Messrs. STANLEY ATHERTON & Co.,
28, Budge Row, London, E.C.

Merrell, Printer, Guide Office, Salcombe.

1909

GOING ONCE
GOING TWICE
GOING WRONG

From as early into the scheme as 1897, several court cases ensued which were heard at the Leeds assizes courts. The Ravenscar Estate Company took several purchasers to court chasing payments for defaulting on their agreements. These defaults were building up, affecting cash flow as well as the viability of the project. Several disgruntled purchasers were objecting to being charged fees for sewerage and roads (which they had to pay extra for connection to) with no sign that they were being put in, other than the initial works. There was also evidence that disgruntled purchasers were trying to sabotage the sales, by pointing out the small print very loudly to potential purchasers. However, sales continued and lots were conveying.
By the end of 1900 there had been thirty-four sales.

Probably at this stage, CENR recognised the situation for himself; plots were selling for less than half of the projected sale figures, the investment prospectus was well off track, no one was actually starting to build, and the promised infrastructure was not going in. He would also have been able to foresee more disgruntled purchasers further down the line. Could this barren piece of land on the top of a cliff, with all the challenges that brought, ever become the new Victorian watering hole he imagined? The plots which he owned were all resold in the sales room (usually at a profit!)

By the mid 1900s the project had all but come to an end. By the end of 1908 the total income from conveyed properties was around £25,000. One common myth is that the Company went bankrupt, abruptly halting the development. In fact, the debenture holders decided to appoint a receiver in 1909 and the Company actually continued to trade in receivership.

The receiver held some further sales but by now there was little interest, although some plots were privately sold and rents continued to be collected, which enabled the debenture holders to be paid some interest.

In 1913 Richard Trolley Hunter purchased land totalling £600 behind what was to have been Derwent Road. In 1919 Frederick Dalby Bulmer of Raven Hall Hotel bought two plots on Roman Road for £500 and two plots on the Pleasaunce / Tan Beck for £135. He bought a further plot on Roman Road in 1921. These plots are where the golf course is now situated. In 1930 seven plots on Pollard Road were sold to Mrs Jessie Smith from Cheshire. In 1939 the hotel purchased two more plots for £35.

In 1947 Raven Hall Hotel reopened for business following its closure due to its requisition by the War Office. The same year the hotel purchased almost a hundred plots for a total of £265. This included the land which now forms the cricket field.

The Town and Country Planning Act of 1947 established that planning permission was required for land development. Ownership alone no longer conferred the right to develop the land. Local authorities were given wide-ranging powers in addition to approval of planning proposals; they could carry out redevelopment of land themselves or use compulsory purchase orders to buy land and lease it to private developers.

The Act provided that all development values were vested in the state, with £300 million set aside for compensation of landowners. Could it have been more than coincidence that the hotel purchased so much land at this time? Did they anticipate the potential for compensation for the newly acquired land? Perhaps the Estate were keen to dispose of the land, knowing that with the passing of the new Act, the right to build on the plots was no longer guaranteed. Whatever the case, none of the newly purchased land was actually built upon.

In 1953 a further twelve plots on Pollard Road and Pollard Place were sold to GL Heppard from Filey for £100.

An Ordnance Survey map from 1960 shows that only six houses had been built since the Estate went into receivership.

By the early seventies, with no further activity or interest in the Estate, it was decided to formerly finish what had begun almost ninety years earlier, and in 1976 what remained of the land was offered to the National Trust for the sum of £4,500. After taking legal advice regarding the receiver's right to sell the land, the National Trust eventually took ownership of this remarkable piece of North Yorkshire history.

THE YORKSHRE EVENING POST THURSDAY DECEMBER 12 1901
THE RAVENSCAR ESTATE VENTURE.
BRADFORD BUILDERS SUED.
VERDICT FOR THE PLAINTIFFS.

At the Leeds Assizes to-day—'before Mr. Justice Grantham and a special jury—'the hearing was resumed of the action brought by the Ravenscar Estate (Ltd.) against William Watkins and Nathan Thompson, builder, both of Bradford, to recover £91 7s., a half yearly instalment, with interest, due on the purchase by them of a plot of land consisting of eight acres 25 perches, from the plaintiff company at Ravenscar, the Yorkshire Coast. Mr. Scott Fox, K.C., and Mr. Shepherd were for the plaintiffs; Mr. Tindal Atkinson, K.C., and Mr. Waugh for the defendants.

The estate consists of about 800 acres and is being developed by the plaintiff company with a view its being made a popular watering place. The defendants purchase took place at an auction sale on September 29, 1899, the price agreed upon being £1,305. deposit of £130 was paid, and it was agreed that the balance, with interest, should paid in half-yearly instalments. Since September 1900, no instalment had been paid.

The defence was that the sale had been affected by misrepresentation, it having been then stated that an efficient system of drainage of the estate would be laid down, whereas, it was contended, no steps had been taken provide any drainage for defendants' property. The defendants therefore asked for the return of their purchase money.

On the other hand, it was stated on behalf of the plaintiffs company that the defendants had never made an application that their land should sewered and had taken no steps to build; and that if they commenced building the directors would be quite willing and prepared to provide drainage for the houses that might erected.

This was substantially the evidence of Mr. C. E. Robinson, barrister, London, one of the directors, who, in cross-examination by Mr. Atkinson, said the estate was bought a syndicate (of which he was a member) for £17,000 £18.000.

At that time the railway station was closed, but it was re-opened, the syndicate sold the estate to the present company for £37,000. He told the judge that the syndicate made no profit in cash but took the whole of their interest in deferred shares.

Mr. Atkinson: You are one 'of the largest shareholders, Mr. Robinson?

Witness: Yes.

The Judge: Made out your briefs, I suppose? (Laughter.)

Witness: made no reply.

Mr. Atkinson: Were not purchasers at these sales constantly demanding from the auctioneer when drainage was to be carried out?

Witness: Yes; there was a regular conspiracy to damage the sales. I think they were great fools coming to us demanding when the drainage was be carried out. . .

But the company had already received £11.000 in hard cash from unfortunate purchasers? —I dare say.

Don't you know that a great many of the purchasers have refused to pay their purchase money in consequence the sewerage scheme not being carried out? — Some of the Bradford people have.

The defendant Thompson, in the course his evidence, stated that he had offered £50 for his bargain on the day he made the purchase, but he declined take it.

His Lordship, in summing up to the jury, said the parties in the case had been two nights and a day trying to settle it, and two days fighting it. As the case was now presented to the jury, it was his duty tell them that they must find a verdict for the plaintiffs. The defendants had withdrawn all charges of fraud and false misrepresentation. The action was purely an action based on fraud and false misrepresentation, and, in his judgment, after having distinctly made these charges people ought not to be allowed to ride off on side issues to endeavour to get a verdict from the jury.

The jury retired to consider their verdict. After an absence of nearly an hour the jury returned with verdict for the plaintiff company, and judgment was given for the amount claimed with costs.

To

THOMAS WILKINSON, *Secretary of The Ravenscar Estate, Limited, 27, Chancery Lane, W.C.*

THE RAVENSCAR ESTATE, LIMITED,
£20,000 MORTGAGE DEBENTURES.

𝔚𝔥𝔢𝔯𝔢𝔞𝔰 𝔚𝔢, BERNARD HARPUR DRAKE, of 24, Rood Lane, in the City of London, Solicitor; EDWARD BOND, of 43, Thurloe Square, S.W., Barrister-at-Law; and CHARLES BOOTH, of 24, Great Cumberland Place, W., Privy Councillor, are the registered holders of a Mortgage Debenture for £500, part of the above issue; AND WHEREAS the said sum of £500 fell due for repayment on the 15th day of October, 1908, and was not then repaid and still remains due to us; AND WHEREAS by Condition 10 of the conditions endorsed on the said Debenture it is provided that the registered holder of such Debenture may with the consent in writing of the holders of the majority in value of the outstanding Debentures of the same series appoint by writing any person or persons to be a Receiver or Receivers of the property charged by the Debentures, and such appointment may be made at any time after the principal moneys thereby secured become payable, and shall be as effective as if all the holders of Debentures of the same series had concurred in such appointment; and that a Receiver or Receivers so appointed shall have power:—

1. To take possession of the property charged by the Debentures.
2. To carry on or concur in carrying on the business of the Company.
3. To sell or concur in selling any of the property charged by the Debentures.
4. To make any arrangement or compromise which they or he shall think expedient in the interests of the Debenture holders.

AND WHEREAS the amount of the Debentures now outstanding is Eight thousand nine hundred and fifty pounds (£8,950). NOW WE, the said BERNARD HARPUR DRAKE, EDWARD BOND, and CHARLES BOOTH, with the consent in writing of the Debenture holders whose names with the amount of their respective holdings are set forth in the Schedule hereto, DO HEREBY APPOINT you the said THOMAS WILKINSON to be Receiver of the property charged by the said Debentures, and to exercise all or any of the powers conferred on the Receiver under and by virtue of the conditions of the said Debenture or by Statute or otherwise.

AS WITNESS our hands this Eighth day of October, One thousand nine hundred and nine.

BERNARD H. DRAKE.

EDWARD BOND.

CHARLES BOOTH.

THE SCHEDULE ABOVE REFERRED TO.

Name of Debenture Holder.	Amount of Holding.
	£
Mrs. Maria Blandy	500
Miss A. C. Bond	300
Rev. John Bond	1,000
Mr. Frank Chaplin	200
Mrs. S. E. L. Cropper	800
Mrs. Jane Cushman	300
Mrs. M. L. Arnold-Forster, Mr. A. H. Loring, and Mr. E. P. Arnold-Forster, Executors of the late Rt. Hon. H. O. Arnold-Forster	200
Miss Annie Kearton	300
Mr. R. J. Lake	450
Mr. N. Story-Maskelyne	2,000
Mrs. E. L. Shute	400
	£6,450

My conclusion is that on the (necessarily) very sketchy facts at present before me I think that <u>the Company would stand a reasonably good chance of establishing a possessory title to these plots</u>. I cannot be more specific than this, however, because at the moment we seem to be in more or less total ignorance of what actually happened when the Company's development plans were halted. Presumably at that stage, either before or after the First World War, there would have been some discussion on what the future of these building plots would be: one would expect the purchasers to have been circularised, by the Company or the receiver, and told what was happening. Was it generally accepted that the purchasers as a whole would do nothing, and in fact abandon their plots? Do not the receiver's records help here?

I would like to have thought that any investigation into these points would be wholly academic, but I do not think that this is so. I notice that in the tenancies correspondence with which I have now been supplied there is to be found reference, dated as recently as <u>1974</u>, to claims by a Mr.Smithson to three plots in Station Road. Apparently he has applied for planning permission and has disputed Mr.Robinson's claim to have a valid tenancy. On 4th March 1974 Mr.Campbell, the receiver, wrote a letter to Mr.Robinson confirming that "some of the plots on the land rented to you belong to persons who purchased them, in some cases as far back as 1902.....". So at least one purchaser, of 3 plots, has not forgotten that he has a documentary title to land now being offered to the Trust.

Advice to National Trust from Donald Nicholls QC. 1976

1920-1976

NO MAN'S LAND

Why was the town never built?

Although there is no definitive answer to this question, there are many factors which may have had an influence.

On some days potential purchasers would arrive by train at Peak, by now known as Ravenscar, and be met by an immaculately manicured Station Square. Greeted by the most stunning views and breath-taking scenery, they could not fail to have been enticed by the prospect of building and owning a property of their dreams and seeing an attainable opportunity to own a home in this wonderful new seaside resort.

On other days, even in the middle of summer, they would have been greeted by sea fret and howling winds from the moors or straight from the North Sea. On those days, it must have seemed a most inhospitable and baron land which was laid out before them.

Walking along Station Road to the sale room at the hotel would give potential purchasers a glimpse of the real Ravenscar which had previously just been a two-dimensional map. The realisation would surely have then struck that there was no sandy beach as drawn on the map, but in its place, there was a very small shingle beach with rocky outcrops, which regularly caused ships to run aground. You had to descend a 600ft cliff, by a winding flight of stairs nearly 2500ft in length, to reach the high-water mark.

Blackpool or Scarborough it was not!

However, people did come from all over the country. There were forty-two auctions held at Ravenscar between 1896 and 1905. One popular myth about this development is that hardly any plots sold. During 42 auction sales 1022 plots were sold under the hammer, which had they all conveyed, should have raised a total of £48,009.94. By 1910, one thousand and twenty-two plots had been sold and six hundred and forty-nine had conveyed, so why were so few houses actually built?!

There was a 'chicken and egg' situation with the infrastructure. The Estate was unwilling to install more sewers until the new plot owners started to build and the plot owners were unwilling to build until there were sewers and water available to connect to.

CENR made a profit on the initial purchase and subsequent sale of the land to the Lands Trading Company and then to the Peak Estate Company. He resold all of the plots which he bought in the early auctions before faith in the scheme dwindled. Raven Hill Hotel was sold but we so far have very little evidence as to what happened to the proceeds of the sale.

According to the sales ledger, the Company had received in excess of £26,000 from sales which had conveyed by 1909. They had also received over £12,000 from the sale of shares. All bank loans and mortgages were paid off, but the debenture holders were never recompensed, although the rents which the receivers continued to collect ensured that they were paid some interest on a regular basis.

We have provided the facts as accurately as we have been able to do so.
There will, undoubtably, be more information which we have as yet not discovered.
The reader must decide for themselves whether or not they feel that the scheme was ever realistically viable and also whether there was a point when the directors should have stopped trying to sell plots. They must have been aware that they were not going to finish the infrastructure. Of course, we are now blessed with the benefit of hindsight!

Answers on a postcard please...!

The steps down to the 'beach' from Station Square

THE RAVE

BALANCE SHEET

1966				
		AUTHORISED CAPITAL		
20,000		2,000 Ordinary Shares of £10 each	20,000. 0. 0.	
20,000		2,000 7% Cumulative Preference Shares of £10 each	20,000. 0. 0.	
£40,000			£40,000. 0. 0.	
		ISSUED CAPITAL		
20,000		2,000 Ordinary Shares of £10 each, fully paid	20,000. 0. 0.	
12,100	32,100	1,200 7% Cumulative Preference Shares of £10 each, fully paid	12,100. 0. 0.	32,100. 0.
		REVENUE RESERVE		
	209	Reserve for dilapidation of land		208. 10.
		DEPOSITS AT 5%	1,448. 5. 2.	
	5,612	add Interest accrued (gross)	4,236. 7. 4.	5,684. 12.
		DEBENTURE AT 5%	1,790. 0. 0.	
	9,706	add Interest accrued (gross)	8,005. 4. 9.	9,795. 4.
		CURRENT LIABILITIES		
105		Debenture Distributions unclaimed	117. 10. 0.	
54	159	Sundry Creditors	73. 5. 3.	190. 15.
	£47,786			£47,979. 2.

ESTATE LIMITED

31st DECEMBER, 1967

1966			
	FIXED ASSETS		
8,490	Estate at cost, less Sales		8,490. 8. 6.
1,753	Expenditure on Sewers at cost, less Assessments received		1,752. 18. 10.
	NOTE:- The above Assets are represented by a few acres of land, which is considered to be of little value.		
	INVESTMENT		
100	Property Owners' Building Society		105. 0. 0.
10,343			10,348. 7. 4.
	CURRENT ASSETS		
47	Sundry Debtors	46. 2. 9.	
186	Cash at Bank	221. 0. 1.	
233			267. 2. 10.
	PROFIT & LOSS ACCOUNT		
37,210	Deficit at 31st December, 1967, per attached Account		37,363. 12. 4.
£47,786			**£47,979. 2. 6.**

And finally, an eloquent view

THE UNBUILT COAST TOWN at RAVENSCAR. (By Peripatetic.)
As printed in the Yorkshire Evening Post 14 August 1913

"It is full summer now." I said to myself as I stepped out of the station. But I had reckoned entirely without considering the weather of Ravenscar, and an icy-cold, wet wind slapped my face by way of contradiction, tore the boater from my head and sent it spinning. When recovered my beloved but battered 'benjie' I went straight back to the booking office and asked the man to give me his winter overcoat and cap and take the straw hat in exchange. "Don't bother to make out ticket'," I said. "It'll be penny all the same," he replied. I paid and he looked unpleasant.

That's the worst of holiday making, one continually parting with pennies. You simply can't take care of the pence, because they will persist in running away to play other people's pockets. As for the pounds taking care of themselves, why, they simply melt away, even though you clasp them in sovereign cases on chains or sew them to your braces. Well, as I turned up the collar of my old well-worn friend of the winter months, and pulled my cap over my ears, I remembered how but a day ago l had basked in the sunshine on the sands at Runswick until old 'Sol' had burnt my nose brown, and now wild, wet, not content with, to speak in sporting parlance, "biting my lugs," had nipped my nose and changed the hue to scarlet. But no matter. Better admit that it is the weather that has painted one's proboscis, than lay a charge against drink or indigestion.

But I anticipate and haven't buttoned my overcoat. . ... There! now, I'm ready to slip out of the station, dare the weather to do its worst, and roam o'er Ravenscar; Yon road I enter upon and look around, I believe you are not all that here, believe that much unseen is also here. Those lines Walt. Whitman sprang to my lip as I walked along. Yes, there must be more in this trim road than meets the eye. This road that leads —where? Other neatly made roads branch off —roads which frankly admit that they lead to nowhere in particular.

The place spreads out before one like a huge draught or chess board, but without the pieces. Here a town has been planned and left unbuilt. One could imagine that was intended to be sort of smug Suburbia-by-the-Sea. But was started exactly the reverse manner to that in which suburbia's spring into existence. There they push up the houses first, and after the inhabitants have had plenty of exercise in walking along planks and old railroad sleepers to avoid the boggy places in reaching their residences, they pay cheerfully towards the cost of the road-making, whereas here the roads are laid ready for the houses. It was almost uncanny to stand there alone on the cliff and survey the land that waits for the town that's yet to be built.

It appeared that I was not the only pebble on the beach, or, rather, blot the skyline, for a man and woman came struggling along, fighting the wind at every step. They stopped, panted for a while, and then said. "Where is the town?" I pointed to the roads. "Isn't there any more of it?" they asked.

"Well," said I, " there's a shop near the station, a church over there, and just past that you'll find such a nice little post office standing in an old-fashioned garden, where long rows of sweet peas grow, and where a cow reclines on patch of green beside the gate, and then there's the fields.

What more do you want?" "We want to find some place where we can get something to eat?" said the man. "Don't all roads here lead to the hotel?" said I.

Then he told of his vain search for food. How they had seen a cottage with board that said, "Refreshments. Teas provided," and when they got there—it was situated in a hollow, away from the road, the cupboard was bare, not a bite to be had or a cup of hot tea to be obtained even for cold cash. "We're going back to the station," he said by way of conclusion. "Haven't you been down to the beach to see the stranded steamer?" I asked. "No, we've been hunting for something to eat all this time," he said, "besides, we've been warned it's a very rough road, and dangerous on such a day as this, so we're going to catch the next train back ' And they turned towards the railway station and I towards the sea. Now, Ravenscar or to be more precise, the site of Ravenscar, stands on a cliff some 700 feet above the sea; at least, the guide book says so, down the slope towards that part which leads to the rough and rugged beach I then accepted that statement as gospel. Had it been said ten times I wouldn't have contradicted it, for when a wild wet wind batters me all the way it feels like 7,000 feet—aye, every inch of it.

I appeared to be the only person passing through the scenery, and a dog in a farmyard spotted me where nearly quarter of a mile separated us, it came forward to meet me in such an unfriendly fashion that I pocketed a few stones with which to welcome this 'friend of man.'

Then it occurred to me that I had read somewhere or other, that if when attacked by savage dog one just sits down smiles, the dog will sit down plead with eloquent eyes that one will scratch its left ear or tickle it under the chin. But I also remember that my friends have frequently complained that mine is a most irritating smile. So, I did not sit down when the too-faithful hound had retired to lick a limb. I went down the side of the cliff and along the beach to where the steamer 'Coronation' rests. It ran ashore there last January and has been an idle ship on the rocky coast ever since. The ship was not deserted, however, and they keep the pot boiling and also sharp look-out see that visitors don't carve their initials on the hull or take away thing as souvenir.

Personally, I think they've been rather un-business like over the whole affair. They might have made money if they had advertised the ideal place for an unconventional holiday. How nice to spend a fortnight upon a stranded ship.

The dog was waiting for me near the top of the cliff and I had to send him away to lick another limb. Evidently it disliked people tramping about there. That reminded me that I hadn't met a solitary tramp in any of the places I had visited on the East Coast, I wondered what a genuine Tired Tim would have thought of Ravenscar. Why? It was hard work to walk about the place.

Just by the hotel I saw a barn-like building board on it which - said, " Bar." I tried the door it was locked. Passing down the yard I saw a cottage, a woman came out to meet me. Hurrah! she possessed the key to the thirst parlour. But alas, that was all she did possess. Not a single biscuit or a crumb of cheese, or even a crust of bread had she to sell. A man might come any moment with cart containing the staff of life. But was it worth while waiting? I decided that it was not.

" I will not roam o'er Ravenscar again until they have erected winter gardens which extend a mile or so. Gardens where lamps ape the sun, and where soft, sweet music of string band soothes one. Where pretty girls sit alone in cosy corners playing 'wallflowers'. Then, and only then, will I take a second glance at Ravenscar, the romantic!

THE UNBUILT COAST TOWN at RAVENSCAR. (By Peripatetic.)
A response: Yorkshire Evening Post 18 August 1913

Sir,
I am surprised at your correspondent's account of Ravenscar. First of all, he arrived on a rainy day. Why did he not remain one night and he would have beheld the very next day glorious with sunshine, pure air, and a magnificent view, and, above all, unlike Scarborough, room to live.
He complains that he could get nothing to eat. Why did he not come on to the hotel, where could have had an excellent dinner. He complains of the dullness of Ravenscar. No pretty girls! No string bands! says your blind correspondent. There are many pretty girls at the hotel, both from your home country and America, but even pretty girls like a rest and holiday from admiration and dress occasionally!
I hope you will keep your string and brass bands to Scarborough, and leave in peace and solitude, from "that madding crowd," to enjoy the magnificence of Ravenscar. As I write, the sun is pouring on to us. We see Robin Hood's Bay below us and have an uninterrupted view on all sides. No houses and chimneys spoil the beautiful broad landscape. Tea on the terrace, and the voices of the happy American girls, who have again crossed the Atlantic this year specially again to visit Ravenscar!
But the less I say of Ravenscar the better, as I want to keep it as is. We do not want your Scarborough crowds. It seems Ravenscar is the only spot left on the East Coast free from commotion.
Yours,

A RAVENSCAR VISITOR.

"A Peripatetic" gave only his own impressions of Ravenscar, and he did not suppose for a moment that everybody would agree with him. We agree with "Ravenscar Visitor" that to have to spend every seaside holiday vouchsafed to us at a fashionable resort where bands and Pierrots prevail would be unutterable boredom. The fashionable resort and quiet Ravenscar each serves its purpose.

Editor.,

The "Coronation" Stranded at Ravenscar.

'Aye'...